Fodor's

Las Vegas'
25Best

by Jackie Staddon and Hilary Weston

Fodor's Travel Publications
New York • Toronto
London • Sydney • Auckland
www.fodors.com

D1005357

How to Use This Book

KEY TO SYMBOLS

➕ Map reference to the accompanying fold-out map

✉ Address

☎ Telephone number

🕐 Opening/closing times

🍴 Restaurant or café

🚆 Nearest rail station

🚝 Nearest monorail station

🚌 Nearest bus/trolley route

⛴ Nearest riverboat or ferry stop

♿ Facilities for visitors with disabilities

❓ Other practical information

▷ Further information

ℹ Tourist information

✋ Admission charges: Very expensive (over $50), Expensive ($20–$50), Moderate ($7–$20), Inexpensive ($7 or less)

★ Major Sight ★ Minor Sight

👣 Walks

🚌 Excursions

🎁 Shops

🎭 Entertainment and Nightlife

🍴 Restaurants

This guide is divided into four sections

• **Essential Las Vegas:** An introduction to the city and tips on making the most of your stay.

• **Las Vegas by Area:** We've broken the city into five areas, and recommended the best sights, shops, entertainment venues, nightlife and restaurants in each one. Suggested walks help you to explore on foot.

• **Where to Stay:** The best hotels, whether you're looking for luxury, budget or something in between.

• **Need to Know:** The info you need to make your trip run smoothly, including getting about by public transportation, weather tips, emergency phone numbers and useful websites.

Navigation In the Las Vegas by Area chapter, we've given each area its own color, which is also used on the locator maps throughout the book and the map on the inside front cover.

Maps The fold-out map accompanying this book is a comprehensive street plan of Las Vegas. The grid on this fold-out map is the same as the grid on the locator maps within the book. We've given grid references within the book for each sight and listing.

Contents

Introducing Las Vegas

Las Vegas is the entertainment capital of the world, where sleep is a mere inconvenience interrupting a continuous stream of fun and hedonism, and where everything is bigger, louder, flashier and trashier than anywhere else in the world.

From the moment you cruise into town it will dawn on you that this is like no other place. The sheer scale of everything is overwhelming, and the Strip (Las Vegas Boulevard South) in all its blazing glory is a thing of wonderment. Where else can you capture a skyscape that includes the Eiffel Tower, St. Mark's Campanile, an Egyptian pyramid and the Statue of Liberty on the same block?

Evolving from the early saloons, the first casinos and hotels were built in the Downtown area in the early 1930s, followed by the expansion of the Strip in the 1940s. So what continues to bring millions of visitors here annually—gambling millions of dollars in the process? Las Vegas is an ever-evolving metropolis with a restless spirit that's part of its electric appeal. Hotels are regularly being torn down to make way for brand-new innovative ideas, and entertainment programs constantly change. Vegas now boasts some of the top restaurants in the world, many run by celebrity chefs, and most top designer names have made their mark on the shopping scene.

You might be forgiven for believing Las Vegas is not synonymous with culture. But beyond the neon there are some great museums and galleries, and ballet and opera blend perfectly with light entertainment. A few miles away from the man-made wonders are dramatic canyons and dams, and sparkling lakes, and the terrain lends itself to some of the finest golf courses. But no matter how you spend your time here, this crazy city will never let you forget that the driving force is gambling. And there is one thing you can gamble on—Vegas once seen is never forgotten.

Facts + Figures

- There are more than 15,000 miles (24,000km) of neon tubing in the Strip and Downtown Las Vegas.
- The casinos make around $26.5 million every day.
- There are more than 175,000 slot machines to take your cash.

RAT PACK MEETS VEGAS

In the 1960s, Las Vegas was dominated by a group of stars collectively known as the Rat Pack. Frank Sinatra first performed at the Sands Hotel in 1960, with John F. Kennedy in the audience. Thereafter, Sinatra, along with Dean Martin, Sammy Davis Jr., Peter Lawford and Joey Bishop—collectively the Rat Pack—dominated the scene and drew the crowds in droves.

TYING THE KNOT IN STYLE

Thousands of people are following in the footsteps of the rich and famous and saying "I do" in Vegas. Famous couples such as Elvis and Priscilla Presley have been joined by Mr. and Mrs. Average from countries as far apart as Britain and Japan, to get married in some of the 50 or so wedding chapels (▷ 77).

HOW IT BEGAN

Spawned from a trading post along the old Spanish Trail, Las Vegas became a popular stop for its freshwater spring. The prospect of gold added to the lure and later the building of the Hoover Dam secured the city's future. The liberal state laws of Nevada allowed the growth of the casinos, and soon the little campsite in the fearsome heat and inhospitable desert developed into a city.

A Short Stay in Las Vegas

DAY 1

Morning Start the day with a leisurely breakfast at the **Rainforest Café** (▷ panel, 42) in the MGM Grand. From here you can be ready and waiting in line at 11am for the opening of the **Lion Habitat** (▷ 28–29) right next door, where you can see the big cats in action.

Mid-morning Cross the walkway to **New York-New York** (▷ 31) to take an exhilarating ride on the Manhattan Express. Head up the Strip to the **Bellagio** (▷ 46) and enjoy the spectacular dancing fountain show before going inside for a spot of culture at the **Bellagio Gallery of Fine Art** (▷ 59).

Lunch Move on to **Caesars Palace** (▷ 47) for lunch at one of the hotel's many superb eating options.

Afternoon Pass through the hotel, trying not to be tempted by the slot machines, to the Forum shops. Partake in some upscale retail therapy under ever-changing skies, and be sure to see the talking statues that come alive throughout the day. Return to the street and take the moving walkway into the **Mirage** (▷ 54–55). The highlight here is the **Dolphin Habitat and the Secret Garden** (▷ 48–49) to the rear of the hotel.

Dinner Proceed to Treasure Island and take the walkway across the Strip to the **Venetian** (▷ 56–57). After a short wander, take an early dinner and soak up the romantic atmosphere in St. Mark's Square.

Evening After dinner, go back over the walkway to try to catch the 7pm showing of the **Sirens of TI** (▷ 61). If the huge crowds deter you, see the volcano erupt into the night sky at the Mirage, then go to a late performance of your favorite show (reserve in advance). After the show, try your luck at the tables until the early hours.

DAY 2

Morning Relax over breakfast at Raffles Café in the **Mandalay Bay** (▷ 112), which has a veranda overlooking the pool area. After you've eaten, visit the hotel's main attraction, **Shark Reef** (▷ 32–33).

Mid-morning Hop on the monorail to the **Excalibur** (▷ 24–25), stopping at Luxor and **King Tut's Tomb** (▷ 26–27) if time allows. Excalibur has some great family entertainment and a fun atmosphere.

Lunch Don't leave the Excalibur without sampling the Roundtable buffet. With your appetite satisfied, cross the walkway to the Tropicana.

Afternoon You should arrive here just in time to see the 2pm showing of **Dirk Arthur's Xtreme Magic** show (▷ 34; not on Friday). Leave the Tropicana and walk past MGM Grand to the **Miracle Mile** (▷ 63) shopping mall—pop in to pick up a few things if you feel the need. Otherwise continue to **Paris Las Vegas** (▷ 53), and take the elevator up the Eiffel Tower for one of the best views of the city. Catch the monorail from here to the **Venetian** (▷ 56), where you can visit two excellent museums, the **Guggenheim** (▷ 50) and **Madame Tussaud's** (▷ 52). To finish the afternoon, treat yourself to a ride on a gondola down the canal.

Dinner Catch the Deuce bus or the Strip trolley downtown to the Queens hotel for a real dining experience at **Hugo's Cellar** (▷ 93); reservations are recommended.

Evening Walk back to Fremont Street to be mesmerized by the **Fremont Street Experience** (▷ 88). After you've seen the show, wander a while and enjoy the party atmosphere, before taking a taxi back to the Strip to join the night owls at a club; try **Studio 54** (▷ 40) or **Tryst** (▷ 81).

Top 25

ESSENTIAL LAS VEGAS TOP 25

These pages are a quick guide to the Top 25, which are described in more detail later. Here they are listed alphabetically and the tinted background shows which area they are in.

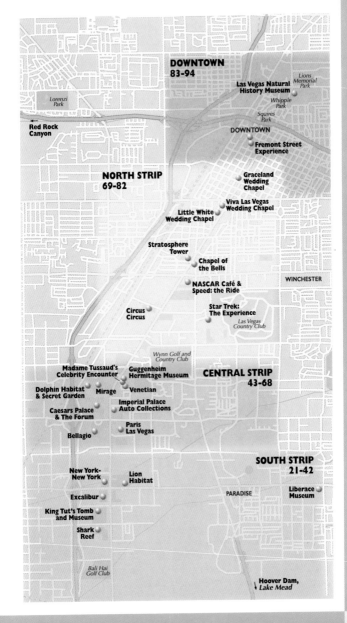

DOWNTOWN
83-94

Las Vegas Natural History Museum

Lions Memorial Park

Whipple Park

Squires Park

Lorenzi Park

Red Rock Canyon

DOWNTOWN

Fremont Street Experience

NORTH STRIP
69-82

Graceland Wedding Chapel

Viva Las Vegas Wedding Chapel

Little White Wedding Chapel

Stratosphere Tower

Chapel of the Bells

WINCHESTER

NASCAR Café & Speed: the Ride

Circus Circus

Star Trek: The Experience

Las Vegas Country Club

Wynn Golf and Country Club

Madame Tussaud's Celebrity Encounter

Guggenheim Hermitage Museum

CENTRAL STRIP
43-68

Dolphin Habitat & Secret Garden

Mirage

Venetian

Caesars Palace & The Forum

Imperial Palace Auto Collections

Paris Las Vegas

Bellagio

New York-New York

Lion Habitat

SOUTH STRIP
21-42

PARADISE

Liberace Museum

Excalibur

King Tut's Tomb and Museum

Shark Reef

Bali Hai Golf Club

Hoover Dam, Lake Mead

9

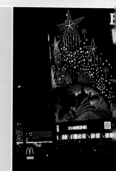

Shopping

Retail therapy in Vegas has soared in recent years, with an influx of designer stores and hundreds of well-known retailers and flag-ship department stores that have put the city firmly on the shopping map. Shopping in Vegas mainly revolves around treading the elegant walkways of the numerous malls. As for choice, it rather depends on how much money you have to spend and how far you are prepared to travel than on what you are looking to buy.

A Unique Experience

Most of the Strip hotels have their own shop-ping opportunities, some more spectacular than others. There is simply no other city in the world where you are able to shop under an arti-ficial sky among Roman architecture and talking statues or journey between shops by gondola, all within a short distance of each other. Hotel malls in Vegas offer more than just great stores: All sorts of entertainment is lined up to amuse you as you shop, but this is reflected in the cost of the goods. There are other malls on the Strip not attached to any particular hotel, such as the huge Fashion Show Mall (▷ 80), where you can browse through the boutiques while a fashion show takes place alongside.

Let's Get Serious

Serious shoppers should venture a few blocks away from the Strip, where they will discover more vast malls that are less crowded, and are

---

PAWNSHOPS

The nature of Vegas means it attracts lots of pawnshops. Many are opposite gambling areas—open 24 hours—ready and waiting to unload desperate gamblers of their possessions for quick cash. Items that are not reclaimed within about 120 days are sold. You will discover all sorts of bizarre items at pawnshops, but jewelry, musical instru-ments and electrical equipment are the most common. Gone are the days of acquiring these items at rock-bottom prices, although you might pick up the odd bargain.

Wynn Esplanade (above middle) is one of many chic hotel malls on offer in Las Vegas

filled with major retailers and specialist stores selling practical items at more realistic prices. Clothes range from daring and trendy to boutique exclusives, and the very latest in shoes, lingerie, jewelry and designer glasses complete a look suitable to hit the Vegas scene. True bargain hunters should head for one of the factory outlets (▷ 92), where top designer clothes, among other things, can be bought at 25–75 percent off. Items for the home, electronics and footwear are particularly good value. A lot of the the merchandise is end of line or last season's items. Just make sure you are getting top-quality and not seconds or damaged goods. Some outlet malls have a shuttle service from hotels on the Strip.

Souvenirs and Gifts

At the other end of the scale from the classy boutiques are the endless souvenir shops along Las Vegas Boulevard, each selling the same mass-produced card decks and key rings. Every hotel also has a gift shop, with logo merchandise that exploits themes to the extreme, while casino gift shops are generally more elegant and expensive. Whether you decide to shop on the Strip or in the malls farther afield, Las Vegas offers its own unique shopping experience that you will not find elsewhere.

THAT SPECIAL GIFT

Although Vegas is not known for one particular souvenir—apart from the kitsch in its gift shops—given the time and money you can buy almost anything here. Gambling merchandise abounds in every guise and quality leather jackets bearing logos are popular. Wine makes a safe gift as Vegas has the largest public collection of fine wines in the world. You might discover that unique collectible you've always wanted—a signed Michael Jordan basketball or autographed Beatles poster. Precious jewels for sale in the city have included Ginger Rogers' engagement ring and the Moghul Emerald (the world's largest carved emerald), but these would break the bank—unless you strike it lucky of course.

There's fabulous retail therapy to be found at Fashion Show Mall (top right) and elsewhere

Shopping by Theme

Whether you're looking for a department store, a quirky boutique, or something in between, you'll find it all in Las Vegas. On this page shops are listed by theme. For a more detailed write-up, see the individual listings in Las Vegas by Area.

ANTIQUES AND COLLECTIBLES

The Attic (▷ 92)
Field of Dreams (▷ 63)
Funk House (▷ 92)
Red Rooster Antiques Mall (▷ 80)
Showcase Slots & Antiques (▷ 64)
Silver Horse Antiques (▷ 92)
Toys of Yesteryear (▷ 92)

BOOKS AND MUSIC

Barnes & Noble (▷ 63)
Gambler's Book Shop (▷ 92)
Sam Ash (▷ 80)

CRAFTS AND SOUVENIRS

Bonanza Gifts (▷ 80)
Chihuly Store (▷ 63)
Danderas (▷ 38)
Dragon's Lair (▷ 38)
Gambler's General Store (▷ 92)
Harley-Davidson (▷ 106)

Las Vegas Paper Dolls (▷ 92)
Liberace Museum Gift Store (▷ 38)
Mikimoto (▷ 63)

FASHION

Bebe (▷ 80)
Betsey Johnson (▷ 80)
Carolina Herrera (▷ 63)
Gianni Versace (▷ 63)
Oscar de la Renta (▷ 80)

FOOD AND WINE

M&M's Academy (▷ 38)
Wine Cellar (▷ 64)

SHOES AND ACCESSORIES

Cowtown Boots (▷ 80)
Jana's Jade Gallery (▷ 106)
Manolo Blahnik (▷ 80)
Pearl Moon Boutique (▷ 38)
Serge's Showgirl Wigs (▷ 80)

SHOPPING MALLS

Boulevard Mall (▷ 106)
Castle Walk (▷ 38)
Chinatown Plaza (▷ 106)
Fashion Show Mall (▷ 80)
Galleria at Sunset (▷ 106)
Giza Galleria (▷ 38)
Grand Canal Shoppes (▷ 63)
Las Vegas Premium Outlets (▷ 92)
Mandalay Place (▷ 38)
Masquerade Village (▷ 63)
Meadows Mall (▷ 106)
Miracle Mile (▷ 63)
Street of Dreams (▷ 38)
Via Bellagio (▷ 64)
Wynn Esplanade (▷ 80)

Las Vegas by Night

Vegas really comes alive after the sun goes down, and some of the best attractions are to be found during the twilight hour. Soak up a pulsating nightlife scene like no other—this is a great place to party.

Endless Variety

From casino lounges to clubs, pubs and cocktail bars, the possibilities for a fun night out are endless. Numerous nightspots provide the chance to dance until dawn. Ultra lounges are the latest trend, stylish spaces that attract a cutting-edge crowd, where DJs spin their vinyl but conversation takes priority. But this is Sin City, and there are several, not very well-concealed, strip joints scattered throughout. These can, however, be disregarded among the sheer scale of everything else.

Only the Best

Las Vegas is infamous for its stage extravaganzas, which incorporate unbelievable special effects, and have attracted some of the world's hottest superstars. Shows vary from Broadway musicals and spectacular productions to comedy and magic. Vegas also plays host to some of the world's biggest special events, such as world championship boxing matches. The top shows can be expensive and the most popular often need to be reserved well in advance. But the best show of all is free: Walk the Strip after dark and be treated to the amazing performance of thousands of flashing neon lights.

Las Vegas is not called the entertainment capital of the world for nothing

GAMING

Where else could you continually be refueled with free drinks as you play the blackjack table or wait for the roulette wheel to stop spinning? But be careful not to lose it all in one night. If you're not a serious player, the slot machines are lots of fun, too. Strolling through the casinos people-watching is another great way to pass the time—weary gamblers desperately trying to claw back some of their losses, and ecstatic cries of joy when their luck holds and the jangling of chips when the slots pay out.

ESSENTIAL LAS VEGAS LAS VEGAS BY NIGHT

Eating Out

Not formerly renowned for good cuisine, Las Vegas has certainly turned things around from the days of lining up for a buffet that focused more on quantity rather than quality.

So What's on Offer?

For starters, the famous Vegas buffet has become much more exciting and provides something for everyone at a reasonable cost. There are endless top-class establishments where you can feast on the superb culinary skills of Michelin-star chefs and there's also the opportunity to dine at a restaurant run by a famous chef. Ever since Wolfgang Puck started the trend here in the 1990s, plenty of new places have opened bearing the names of celebrity chefs. The sheer variety of cuisine that has emerged is astonishing, from Italian and Mexican to Mediterranean, Indian and Pacific Rim. Fast-food outlets still play an important role, as do traditional steak houses.

Dining Tips

It can be hard to get a table at high-end restaurants, especially on Friday and Saturday nights. Plan ahead—you can reserve up to 30 days in advance. Many of these open for dinner only. Mid-range eateries are more likely to be open all day, and you will not need a reservation for breakfast or lunch. Most major hotels have a fast-food court to grab a quick bite, and many have a buffet at breakfast, lunch and dinner. Buffet lines can be long so allow plenty of time.

DINNER SHOWS

If your time is short in Las Vegas you might like to take advantage of one of the dinner shows on offer, where you can eat and be thoroughly entertained at the same time. Probably the most popular of these is Tournament of Kings at the Excalibur (▷ 24). Also making headlines is Tony 'n' Tina's Wedding at the Rio (✉ 3700 West Flamingo Road ☎ 702/777-7777 🕐 Daily 7pm), a wild-and-wacky show in which you are invited to join Tony and Tina for their wedding feast.

Restaurants have evolved into an attraction in themselves with a Las Vegas flavor

Restaurants by Cuisine

There are restaurants to suit all tastes and budgets in Las Vegas. On this page they are listed by cuisine. For a more detailed description of each restaurant, see Las Vegas by Area.

BUFFETS

Bay Side (▷ 41)
Bellagio Buffet (▷ 66)
Big Kitchen (▷ 66)
Carnival World (▷ 66)
Garden Court (▷ 93)
Paradise Garden Buffet (▷ 68)

CAFÉS AND PUBS

Binion's Coffee Shop (▷ 93)
Chocolate Swan (▷ 41)
Harley Davidson Café (▷ 67)
Il Fornaio Panetteria (▷ 42)
Tilted Kilt (▷ 68)
Verandah High Tea (▷ 42)

FRENCH AND OTHER EUROPEAN

Brasserie Boulud (▷ 82)
Bouchon (▷ 66)
Drai's (▷ 67)
Hugo's Cellar (▷ 93)
Mon Ami Gabi (▷ 68)
Picasso (▷ 68)
Pietro's (▷ 42)
Red Square (▷ 42)
Top of the World (▷ 82)

ITALIAN

Andiamo (▷ 82)
Battista's Hole in the Wall (▷ 66)
Canaletto (▷ 66)
Francesco's (▷ 67)
Valentino (▷ 68)

NORTH AMERICAN AND MEXICAN

Aureole (▷ 41)
Border Grill (▷ 41)
Bradley Ogden (▷ 66)
Dona Maria Tamales (▷ 93)
Emeril's (▷ 41)
House of Lords (▷ 67)
Postrio (▷ 68)
Toto's (▷ 42)

ORIENTAL/FUSION

China Grill (▷ 41)
Fusia (▷ 41–42)
Hyakumi (▷ 67)
Kokomo's (▷ 67)
Lillie's Noodle House (▷ 93)
Lotus of Siam (▷ 82)

STEAKS AND SEAFOOD

Noodle Shop (▷ 42)
Ra (▷ 82)
Second Street Grill (▷ 93)
Binion's Ranch Steakhouse (▷ 93)
Charlie Palmer Steak (▷ 41)
Envy (▷ 82)
Kristofer's (▷ 82)
Lawry's The Prime Rib (▷ 67)
Limericks (▷ 93)
Michael Mina (▷ 67)
Nero's (▷ 68)
Nobhill (▷ 42)
The Steakhouse (▷ 82)
Village Seafood (▷ 68)

If You Like...

However you'd like to spend your time in Las Vegas, these top suggestions should help you tailor your ideal visit. Each sight or listing has a fuller write-up in Las Vegas by Area.

SOMETHING FOR FREE

You can't help but be drawn to the spectacular Bellagio Fountains (▷ 46).
Take a trip downtown to see the Fremont Street Experience (▷ 88), a dazzling display of images cast on an LED-light roof.
Visit one of the free live animal attractions, such as the Lion Habitat (▷ 28–29) at MGM Grand.

GETTING THE HEART PUMPING

Great for an adenalin rush, brave the thrill rides atop the Stratosphere Tower (▷ 76).
The Manhattan Express (▷ 31) and Speed (▷ 74) will provide an exhilarating experience.
Take to the sky in a helicopter or small plane for a bird's-eye-view of the Hoover Dam (▷ 98).

The Stratosphere Tower (above); Fremont ablaze (top)

TO HIT THE SHOPPING MALLS

At Fashion Show Mall (▷ 80) you will find all the leading US department stores and lots more.
For a true smorgasbord of shopping deals, head for the outlet malls (▷ 92).
Entertainment and retail therapy go hand-in-hand at Miracle Mile (▷ 63).

DINING IN A ROMANTIC SETTING

Dine at Mon Ami Gabi (▷ 68), within view of the Bellagio fountains.
106 floors up, the revolving Top of the World (▷ 82) offers the best views of the city and good food, too.
Enjoy Italian food at Canaletto (▷ 66), over-looking Venice's St. Mark's Square.

Fashion Show Mall (above right); dinner in St. Mark's Square (right)

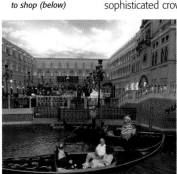

Limos and luxury dining are part of the Las Vegas scene (below)

TO BE PAMPERED

Travel from the airport to your hotel in a stretch limousine or Hummer (▷ 119).
Check in at one of Las Vegas' most luxurious resorts, like the Bellagio (▷ 46).
Indulge yourself in ultimate pampering at the Spa (▷ 61) at Caesars Palace.

DELECTABLE HOT SPOTS

Dine in restaurants created by celebrity chefs—try Bradley Ogden at Caesar's Palace (▷ 66), Michael Mina (▷ 67) at Bellagio and Thomas Keller's Bouchon (▷ 66) at the Venetian.
Take advantage of some of the city's finest French cuisine; Brasserie Boulud (▷ 82) is one of the best.
For a sweet finish to your culinary tour, have dessert at the Chocolate Swan at Mandalay Bay (▷ 41).

HIGH-ENERGY DANCE CLUBS

Show your moves on one of the four dance floors at Studio 54 (▷ 40).
Join the super chic at Risqué (▷ 65) lost in the pulsating music.
For new innovations that will impress join the sophisticated crowd at Tryst (▷ 81).

The Grand Canal mall, what a wonderful way to shop (below)

RESORT SHOPPING

Sample unique shopping under an artificial sky at the Forum (▷ 47).
You will almost believe you are in Venice at the Grand Canal Shoppes (▷ 63).
Find a classy and distinctive collection of designer shops at the Wynn Esplanade (▷ 80).

ESSENTIAL LAS VEGAS IF YOU LIKE...

Amazing shows, thrilling rides or a spot of pampering, take your pick

WORLD-CLASS ENTERTAINMENT

See a Broadway production: Phantom of the Opera is the latest to arrive on the scene at the Venetian (▷ 56–57).

Reserve well in advance for a close encounter with a megastar; check out the Colosseum (▷ 64) to see who's making headlines.

Be amazed by one of the many Cirque du Soleil (▷ 65) productions in town.

TO TAKE THE KIDS ALONG

Visit Circus Circus (▷ 72–73), the only gaming establishment that caters for children and adults.

The animal attractions at the Mirage (▷ 54–55) will enchant the whole family.

Children will never get bored at the Excalibur (▷ 24–25), a fantasyland of fun and games inside a sparkling castle.

NON GAMING-HOTELS

Stay within the plush sanctuary of the Four Seasons at Mandalay Bay (▷ 112).

The Alexis Park (▷ 110) provides a tranquil oasis just minutes from the action.

For state-of-the-art amenities without the gambling, the Renaissance (▷ 112) fits the bill.

You pays your money, you takes your chances (below)

SOME CASINO ACTION

Join the high rollers at the Venetian (▷ 56–57), watched over by Tiepolo's and Titian's.

Cocktail waitresses in togas will serve you drinks at Caesars (▷ 47) while you place your bets.

Tuxedo-backed chairs set the tone at New York-New York (▷ 31), set against the backdrop of the Big Apple.

SOUTH STRIP

CENTRAL STRIP

NORTH STRIP

DOWNTOWN

FARTHER AFIELD

Until 1990 this end of the Strip was little more than the "Welcome to Las Vegas" sign. Now the skyline is unrecognizable, with the addition of a pyramid and the Statue of Liberty, among other things.

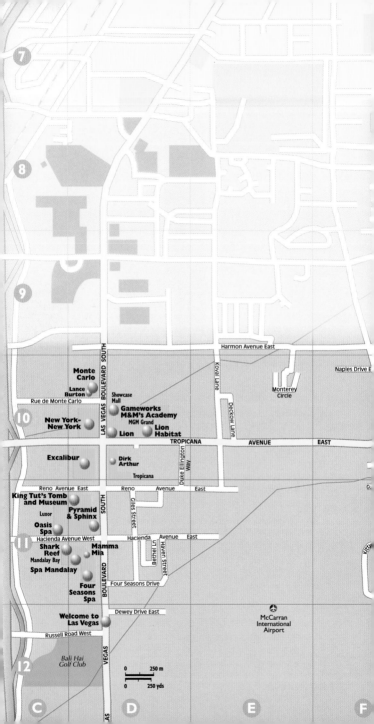

7

8

9

Harmon Avenue East

Naples Drive E

Monte Carlo

Lance Burton

Rue de Monte Carlo

Showcase Mall

Gameworks M&M's Academy

MGM Grand

Monterey Circle

Deckow Lane

Koval Lane

10

New York-New York

Lion

Lion Habitat

TROPICANA   AVENUE   EAST

Excalibur

Dirk Arthur

Tropicana

Duke Ellington Way

Reno Avenue East

Reno   Avenue   East

King Tut's Tomb and Museum

Pyramid & Sphinx

Luxor

Giles Street

Oasis Spa

Hacienda Avenue West

Hacienda   Avenue   East

11

Shark Reef

Mamma Mia

Mandalay Bay

Bethel Ln

Haven Street

KIRK

Spa Mandalay

Four Seasons Spa

Four Seasons Drive

Welcome to Las Vegas

Dewey Drive East

Russell Road West

McCarran International Airport

12

Bali Hai Golf Club

LAS VEGAS BOULEVARD SOUTH

VEGAS

0   250 m
0   250 yds

C   **D**   **E**   **F**

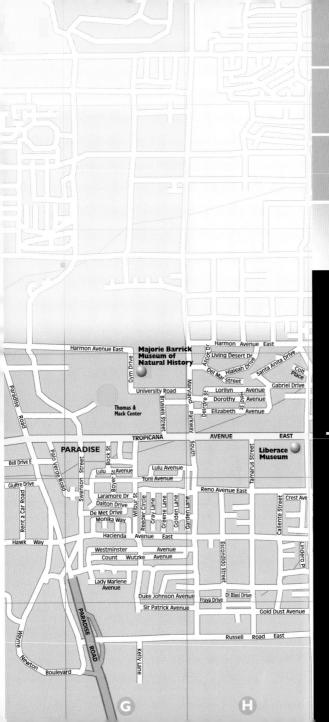

Harmon Avenue East

Majorie Barrick Museum of Natural History

Harmon Avenue East

Gym Drive

Ascot Dr

Living Desert Dr

Del Mar Street

Hialeah Drive

Santa Anita Drive

Colt Place

University Road

Maryland

Brussels Street

Del Dre St

Lorilyn Avenue

Dorothy Avenue

Elizabeth Avenue

Gabriel Drive

Paradise Road

Thomas & Mack Center

Parkway

Bell Drive E

Giuffre Drive

Rent a Car Road

TROPICANA

South

AVENUE

EAST

Tamarus Street

Liberace Museum

PARADISE

Swenson Street

Palo Verde Road

Bock St.

Boyer

Lulu Avenue

Lulu Avenue

Toni Avenue

Reno Avenue East

Callente Street

Crest Ave

Laramore Dr

Dalton Drive

De Met Drive

Monika Way

Wilbur St

Reeder Circle

Cray Lane

Greene Lane

Golden Lane

Garden Lane

Hawk Way

Hacienda Avenue East

Westminster Avenue

Count Wutzke Avenue

Escondido Street

Lady Marlene Avenue

Duke Johnson Avenue

Sir Patrick Avenue

Fraya Drive

Di Blasi Drive

Gold Dust Avenue

Linpero Dr

PARADISE ROAD

Wayne

Newton

Boulevard

Kelly Lane

Russell Road East

G

H

Excalibur

**All the romance and excitement of
legendary medieval Europe is re-created
at this sparkling castle-shaped hotel, with
exciting special effects, sword fights,
jousting and jugglers.**

Camelot Cross the drawbridge and you enter a
world where technology meets the legend of King
Arthur. Inside the stone walls, stained glass and
heraldic shields set the scene, and strolling performers dressed in costumes enhance the atmosphere.

Medieval Village An escalator transports you to
the second floor, where you are greeted by a fire-
breathing dragon. The main stage presents free
shows, including juggling, puppetry and storytelling.
On the lower level at the Fantasy Faire Midway
there are traditional carnival attractions, state-of-the-

Fun, food and a battle royal at Tournament of Kings (left); King Arthur would feel right at home under the turrets of the Excalibur (right); illuminated at night (middle, bottom left); a feast to behold, the round-table buffet (bottom right)

art video games and Merlin's Magic Motion simulator rides. Shops sell medieval-style merchandise, and there are several theme restaurants.

Tournament of Kings This enthralling show revolves around highly skilled stunts—often on horseback—high-tech special effects, wonderful costumes and a stirring musical score. King Arthur and his knights play host to other monarchs across Europe. There's a procession, followed by traditional medieval games of skill, agility, might and endurance. But when the evil Mordred attacks, amid burning fires and accompanied by a dragon, the clash of swords begins. The victor is presented with Excalibur by Merlin and the show ends with more festivities. While pulling apart their chicken dinner with greasy hands, the audience is involved in partisan support during the jousting.

THE BASICS

www.excalibur-casino.com

🔲 D10

✉ 3850 Las Vegas Boulevard South

☎ 702/597-7777.
Tournament of Kings:
702/597-7600

🕐 Tournament of Kings:
Fri–Mon, Wed 6 and
8.30pm, Thu 6pm

🍴 Several cafés and restaurants

🚌 Deuce; Strip trolley

💲 Tournament of Kings:
very expensive. Merlin's
Magic Motion rides:
inexpensive

King Tut's Tomb and Museum

HIGHLIGHTS

● The golden tomb
● Replica gold-plated sarcophagus
● The museum shop, where authentic Egyptian art is on sale

TIP

● The self-guiding audio tour is independent of other visitors so you can take it any time you choose.

With its Egyptian theme and pyramid architecture, what else could the Luxor do but reproduce the glittering bounty of Egypt's most famous king and his renowned burial treasures?

"I see wonderful things" These were the words of British archaeologist Howard Carter when he discovered the fabled tomb of Tutankhamun in 1922. It was the greatest archaeological find of all time, the most intact tomb ever discovered in the Valley of the Kings (just outside the town of Luxor in Egypt) and took 10 years to excavate. In contrast, the Luxor hotel replicated the tomb in its Pharaoh Pavilion in just six months. Even so, this is no tacky imitation. The replicas exhibited in the museum were faithfully created by craftsmen in Egypt, using traditional methods and tools that were employed thousands

Take an exciting trip down the Nile at this museum filled with reproduction objects from Luxor in Egypt, with King Tutankhamun's tomb stealing the show

of years ago, and incorporating authentic materials such as gold leaf and precious pigments. It is the only exhibit of its kind outside of Egypt.

Museum tour It takes 15 minutes to follow the self-guiding audio tour of the museum, and it's a breathtaking quarter-hour. The entire layout of King Tutankhamun's tomb has been exactly re-created under the direction of renowned Egyptologist Dr. Omar Mabreuck. The focus is, of course, the sarcophagus of the young king and the illustrious guardian statues that watched over his last resting place. The original tomb consisted of nine outer cases protecting the mummified remains, and the innermost one was made of solid gold. There are also beautifully crafted figurines and wall paintings, and subdued lighting casts an atmospheric golden glow over the entire exhibit.

THE BASICS

www.luxor.com

✚ D11

✉ Luxor, 3900 Las Vegas Boulevard South

☎ 702/262-4444

🕐 Daily 10–11

🍴 Cafés and restaurants at Luxor

🚌 Deuce; Strip trolley

♿ Moderate

Lion Habitat

HIGHLIGHTS

● Having a photo taken with one of the cubs
● Watching the trainers interact with the lions

TIPS

● The line for photos can be very long; you can bypass it and just walk through.
● The gift shop has some adorable stuffed toys for sale.

This is a remarkable place, where you can get up close to magnificent big cats in the happy knowledge that their stay in the enclosure will be only slightly longer than yours.

A temporary sojourn Anyone who has qualms about wild animals being caged for human entertainment can rest assured that the lions are brought here for just a short time from their spacious home outside the city. They belong to animal trainer Keith Evans, who makes the trip three times a day to ensure that no cat is in the enclosure for longer than six hours.

Surrounded by lions The three-level structure, reaching a height of more than 35ft (10m), is similar in concept to the walk-through tunnels

Have a rip-roaring time observing these elegant creatures in their glass enclosure

you'll find in big aquariums. You will see the animals close up, and can study their every move with perfect clarity as they prowl on either side and even stride across the tunnel roof above your head—and all that separates you is a thick layer of the toughest strengthened glass available. The Lion Habitat has been laid out to resemble the natural landscape the cats would know in the wild, including indigenous foliage, rocks, four separate waterfalls and a pond.

Raised in captivity One of the most famous lions of all time was Metro, whose roar announced every MGM Studio production. Three of his descendants—Goldie, Metro and Baby Lion—are among the collection of more than two dozen big cats, all of which have been raised in captivity by Evans and his wife at their 8-acre (3ha) estate.

THE BASICS

www.mgmgrand.com

⊞ D10

✉ MGM Grand, 3799 Las Vegas Boulevard South

☎ 702/891-7777

🕐 Daily 11–10

🍽 Cafés and restaurants at MGM Grand

🚇 MGM Grand

🚌 Deuce; Strip trolley

✋ Free

Liberace Museum

TOP 25

What a showman (left); welcome to Liberace's world (middle); his prized Rolls-Royce (right)

THE BASICS

www.liberace.org

✚ H10

✉ 1775 East Tropicana Avenue, at Spencer

☎ 702/798-5595

🕐 Tue–Sat 10–5, Sun 12–4

🚍 201

♿ Moderate

HIGHLIGHTS

● Concert piano collection
● Rolls-Royce collection
● Costumes, including a black diamond mink cape and the famous red, white and blue hot-pants suit
● Candelabra ring
● Precious stone collection
● Re-creation of Palm Springs bedroom

Outrageous and ostentatious—a testament to bad taste and kitsch. This statement could easily be used as a slogan for Las Vegas city, but here it refers to just one collection, the incredible Liberace Museum.

Setting the scene From the moment you see the fluorescent pink entrance sign, you are drawn into the world of one of the most extraordinary entertainers of the 20th century. This shrine to the legend of "Mr Showmanship" is as outrageous as Liberace himself. The museum, the legacy of the world's highest-paid musician, was founded by Liberace in 1977 as a nonprofit organization. On show are vintage pianos and cars, exuberant costumes, glitzy jewelry and a host of memorabilia.

From classical beginnings Born in the US in 1919 of Italian/Polish parents, Wladziu Liberace had a classical training and made his debut with the Chicago Symphony at the age of 14. In 1955 he opened at the Riviera as the highest-paid entertainer in the city's history, his flamboyant style always attracting attention. He died in 1987.

Antiques to kitsch To the rippling tones of Liberace's keyboard artistry you can view an amazing collection of pianos, including rare antiques. Check out the rhinestone-encrusted Baldwin grand and Liberace's favorite, covered entirely in glittering mirror squares. See the superb bejeweled Rolls-Royces, sequined, feathered and rhinestone-studded costumes, and a glittering array of jewelry, including the trademark candelabra ring.

But surely we must be in New York (left). The ups and downs of life in New York (right)

New York-New York

See the sights of the Big Apple in a fraction of the time needed to explore the real thing. The Statue of Liberty, Brookyn Bridge, the Chrysler Building—they are all here.

New York in miniature Standing 47 floors high, this resort hotel claims to be the tallest in Nevada. The New York skyline is depicted through scaled-down replicas—about one-third of the actual size—of famous city landmarks. The Statue of Liberty keeps watch over the Strip side by side with sky-scrapers such as the Empire State Building and a 300ft-long (91m) version of the Brooklyn Bridge.

Manhattan Express A thrilling roller coaster twists, loops and dives at speeds of up to 67mph (97kph) around the skyscrapers to a height of 203ft (62m). Your whole world literally turns upside down and inside out when the train drops 144ft (44m). This ride was the first ever to introduce the "heartline" twist and dive move, where riders experience weightlessness—the train rolls 180 degrees, suspending its passengers 86ft (26m) above the casino roof, before taking a sudden dive.

Behind the scenes The hotel's art deco lobby is set against representations of Times Square, Little Italy and Wall Street, and the casino is modeled on Central Park. A selection of restaurants and shops also follows the theme. Upstairs, the Coney Island Emporium re-creates the atmosphere of an early-1900s amusement park alongside the latest video technology at ESPN Zone.

THE BASICS

www.nynyhotelcasino.com

🔢 D10

✉ 3790 Las Vegas Boulevard South

☎ 702/740-6969

🕐 Manhattan Express: Sun–Thu 11–11, Fri, Sat 11–midnight

🍴 Several cafés and restaurants

🚇 MGM Grand

🚌 Deuce; Strip trolley

♿ Manhattan Express: moderate

❓ You must be 54in (1.38m) to ride the roller coaster

HIGHLIGHTS

● Manhattan Express
● Statue of Liberty
● Brooklyn Bridge
● ESPN Zone

Shark Reef

HIGHLIGHTS

- Sharks up to 12ft (3.5m) long
- Back Reef Tunnel
- Talking to the naturalists
- Touch pool
- Golden crocodiles

TIP

- A self-guiding audio tour is included in the price, with cards to help you identify the fish.

A hundred different species of shark, plus other magnificent aquatic creatures, can be encountered close up in the imaginatively re-created marine environments of this aquarium.

Massive tanks Shark Reef covers more than 91,000sq ft (8,450sq m) and its tanks—arranged in 14 main exhibits—contain an incredible 1.6 million gallons (7.2 million liters) of mineral-rich reconstituted sea water. It's home to more than 2,000 species of marine creatures—not only the sharks, but also sea turtles, reptiles and fish.

The major exhibits In Treasure Bay, a sunken ship sits on the bed of a lagoon, circled by four kinds of shark. Shoals of snapper and jack dart around, in contrast to the laid-back gliding of the two green

Visitors marvel at the marine life in Mandalay Bay—lionfish (top left), bonnethead shark (top middle), stingray (below right)—to name a few

sea turtles. The experience of diving on a coral reef is re-created in the Back Reef Tunnel, whose water is full of bright tropical fish to the left, right and above you, and there is every probability of coming nose to nose with bonnethead sharks. Elsewhere, you will see rays skimming through the water or resting on the ocean floor.

Reptiles, amphibians and jungle flora Rare golden crocodiles inhabit the Crocodile Habitat (the only place in the western hemisphere where you can see them), and in the Lizard Lounge there are huge water monitor lizards up to 9ft (2.7m) in length. The Serpents and Dragons exhibit, separated from curious onlookers by only a pool of water, houses venomous snakes and the Australian Arowana dragon fish. The Temple exhibits offer a refreshing rain-forest experience.

THE BASICS

www.mandalaybay.com
🔳 C11
✉ Mandalay Bay, 3950 Las Vegas Boulevard South
☎ 702/632-7777 or 702/632-4555
🕐 Daily 10–11; last admission 10
🍴 Cafés and restaurants at Mandalay Bay
🚌 Deuce; Strip trolley
♿ Moderate

More to See

DIRK ARTHUR: XTREME MAGIC

www.tropicanalv.com

It's magic to the extreme, with revolutionary magician Dirk Arthur's fast-paced show interweaving dance, breathtaking magic and exotic animals.

✚ D10 ✉ Tropicana, 3801 Las Vegas Boulevard South ☎ 702/739-2222 🕐 Sat–Thu 2 and 4pm 🚇 MGM Grand 🚌 Deuce; Strip trolley ✋ Expensive

FOUR SEASONS SPA

www.fourseasons.com/lasvegas

This is an exquisite facility for the ultimate pampering. Treatments include facials, body scrubs, massages and mud treatments, and there are two private spa suites, with sauna, steam room, whirlpool tub and massage table. The fitness suite includes weights and cardiovascular equipment, saunas, steam rooms and Jacuzzis, and there's a jogging track through the beautiful grounds.

✚ D11 ✉ Four Seasons, 3960 Las Vegas Boulevard South ☎ 702/632-5302 🕐 Daily 8–7 🚌 Deuce; Strip trolley

GAMEWORKS

www.gamesworks.com

A creation from movie mogul Steven Spielberg that is the ultimate in interactive, virtual-reality arcade games; it is geared mostly to teenagers.

✚ D10 ✉ Showcase Mall, 3785 Las Vegas Boulevard South ☎ 702/432-4263 🕐 Sun–Thu 10am–midnight, Fri, Sat 10am–1am 🚇 MGM Grand 🚌 Deuce; Strip trolley ✋ Admission free; individual activities inexpensive

LANCE BURTON: MASTER MAGICIAN

www.montecarlo.com

A fascinating display of the illusionist's art, plus traditional sleight-of-hand tricks that leave the audiences gasping. A good family show.

✚ D10 ✉ Monte Carlo, 3770 Las Vegas Boulevard South ☎ 702/730-7777 🕐 Tue–Sat 7pm (also Tue, Sat 10pm) 🚌 301, 302; Strip trolley ✋ Very expensive

THE LION OUTSIDE MGM

Unlike its live counterparts inside the MGM Grand (▷ 28–29), this

Sheer heaven at the Four Seasons Spa

Lance Burton conjures up a magic moment

sedentary lion is made of bronze, is 45ft (14m) tall and weighs in at 100,000 lb (45,360kg). It represents MGM Studios' signature lion, Metro.

➕ D10 ✉ MGM Grand, 3799 Las Vegas Boulevard South 🚇 MGM Grand 🚌 Deuce; Strip trolley

MAMMA MIA!

www.mamma-mia.com

Attracting rave reviews wherever in the world it is staged, this show combines the story of a mother and daughter, the daughter's three possible fathers and a memorable wedding with the music of Swedish supergroup ABBA. Reservations usually required. (Due to close end of 2008.)

➕ C11 ✉ Mandalay Bay, 3950 Las Vegas Boulevard South 🕿 702/632-7777 🕐 Sun–Thu 7pm, Sat 6 and 10 🚌 Deuce; Strip trolley 💷 Expensive

MARJORIE BARRICK MUSEUM OF NATURAL HISTORY

www.hrcweb.nevada.edu/museum

Less than 3 miles (5km) from the Strip on the university campus is this

excellent museum devoted to the Native Americans of the region, the wildlife and also the history of ancient Mesoamerica.

➕ G10 ✉ 4505 South Maryland Parkway 🕿 702/895-3381 🕐 Mon–Fri 8–4.45, Sat 10–2 🚌 109 💷 Free

M&M'S ACADEMY

www.m-ms.com

An interactive shopping and retail complex over four floors with thousands of M&M's brand merchandise items, plus a 3-D movie theater, an M&M's Racing Team store and a wall covered in a multitude of different colored plain and peanut M&Ms.

➕ D10 ✉ Showcase Mall, 3785 Las Vegas Boulevard South 🕿 702/736-7611or 702/740-2504 🕐 Sun–Thu 9am–11pm, Fri, Sat 9–midnight 🚇 MGM Grand 🚌 Deuce; Strip trolley 💷 Admission free; movie inexpensive

MONTE CARLO

www.montecarlo.com

Fanciful arches, chandeliered domes, ornate fountains and gaslit promenades set the scene at this resort

The sweet taste of success at M&M's

Monte Carlo or bust

hotel modeled on the Place du Casino in Monte Carlo. The master illusionist Lance Burton (▷ 34), has been here for a number of record-breaking years.

🚩 D10 ✉ 3770 Las Vegas Boulevard South ☎ 702/730-7777 🚌 Deuce; Strip trolley

OASIS SPA
www.luxor.com
The only place in Vegas where you can have a relaxing massage or other treatment in the early hours after a night on the town. A whole range of exercise equipment—treadmills, bicycles, weight machines, climbing machines—is available here, along with such treatments as body wraps, body scrubs, massages, hydrotherapy and facials. There are tanning beds, too.

🚩 C11 ✉ Luxor, 3900 Las Vegas Boulevard South ☎ 702/730-5724 ◷ Daily 24 hours 🚌 Deuce; Strip trolley

PYRAMID AND SPHINX
www.luxor.com
A gigantic black-glass pyramid, complete with a massive 10-floor replica sphinx guarding its entrance,

dominates the Luxor. With its high-intensity lights, the pyramid is actually visible from space.

🚩 D11 ✉ Luxor, 3900 Las Vegas Boulevard South 🚌 Deuce; Strip trolley

SPA MANDALAY
www.mandalaybay.com
This opulent facility has picture windows with a wonderful view over the hotel's lagoon and gardens. In addition to traditional treatments, there is a range of more exotic techniques, including ayurvedic relaxation and Swedish massage, while amenities include whirlpools with waterfalls, saunas and Swedish showers.

🚩 D11 ✉ Mandalay Bay, 3950 Las Vegas Boulevard South ☎ 702/632-7220 ◷ Daily 8–9 🚌 Deuce; Strip trolley

WELCOME TO FABULOUS "LAS VEGAS" SIGN
Designed in 1959, this famous sign welcomes you as you enter Las Vegas at the south end of the Strip.

🚩 D12 ✉ Las Vegas Boulevard South 🚌 Deuce

Just in case you need to be reminded where you are

Come inside and spoil yourself at Spa Mandalay

Shopping

CASTLE WALK
Well and truly carrying on the medieval theme, this mall includes Merlin's Mystic Shoppe, selling magic tricks and accoutrements, a medieval hatter, and a place where you can buy replica swords and shields (and the occasional suit of armor).
➕ D10 ✉ Excalibur, 3850 Las Vegas Boulevard South ☎ 702/597-7850 🚌 Deuce; Strip trolley

DANDERAS
Luxor's line of spa products is sold exclusively at this bath and body shop. Also candles, aromatherapy products and jewelry.
➕ D11 ✉ Giza Galleria, Luxor, 3900 Las Vegas Boulevard South ☎ 702/262-4970 🚌 Deuce; Strip trolley

DRAGON'S LAIR
This is the place for full-size replicas of swords, shields and the odd suit of armor. More portable souvenirs include crystals, dragon sculptures and Merlin figurines.
➕ D10 ✉ Excalibur, 3850 Las Vegas Boulevard South ☎ 702/597-7850 🚌 Deuce; Strip trolley

GIZA GALLERIA
This Egyptian-theme mall includes both genuine and reproduction antiques, as well as kids' clothing and toys and cosmetics.
➕ D11 ✉ Luxor, 3900 Las Vegas Boulevard South

☎ 702/262-4970 🚌 Deuce; Strip trolley

LIBERACE MUSEUM GIFT STORE
www.liberace.org
For ardent Liberace fans, among the souvenirs for sale are Liberace-theme items, CDs, music-related books, giftware, stationery and jewelry.
➕ H10 ✉ 1775 Tropicana Avenue East ☎ 702/798-5595 🚌 201

M&M'S ACADEMY
www.m-ms.com
A tourist attraction as well as a candy store, this place has a huge selection of well-known confectionery brands, including a vast array of liqueur-filled chocolates

HOTEL SHOPPING
You will find many familiar stores in hotel malls, such as Gap, Victoria's Secret, Tommy Bahama and Levi's Original, and the classier places will have designer boutiques like Prada and Hermès, too. You won't find the big department stores here, but you'll be able to buy a good range of items, including more mundane requirements such as toiletries, cosmetics and magazines. Souvenirs may include pieces that reflect the hotel's theme, or merchandise from the permanent shows and visiting entertainers.

and, of course, M&M's.
➕ D10 ✉ Showcase Mall, 3785 Las Vegas Boulevard South ☎ 702/736-7611 🚌 Deuce; Strip trolley

MANDALAY PLACE
A sky bridge connecting Mandalay Bay with the Luxor is home to a number of superior retailers. These include a good Mamma Mia show souvenir shop, a swimwear boutique, a shop selling hand-carved Balinese furniture and an excellent florist.
➕ D11 ✉ Mandalay Bay, 3950 Las Vegas Boulevard South ☎ 702/632-6753 🚌 Deuce; Strip trolley

PEARL MOON BOUTIQUE
It's a bit on the pricey side, but the selection of swimwear, hats, sunglasses and sandals here is better quality than you'll find at other shops on the Strip.
➕ D11 ✉ Mandalay Bay, 3950 Las Vegas Boulevard South ☎ 702/632-6753 🚌 Deuce; Strip trolley

STREET OF DREAMS
A modest mall with clothing boutiques, plus the fascinating Lance Burton Magic Shop, with souvenirs and magic tricks to remind you of the master illusionist's show (▷ 34).
➕ D10 ✉ Monte Carlo, 3770 Las Vegas Boulevard South ☎ 702/730-7502 🚌 Deuce; Strip trolley

Entertainment and Nightlife

BALI HAI GOLF CLUB
www.balihaigolfclub.com
A South Pacific theme pervades throughout this 18-hole course, with outcrops of volcanic rock, groups of palm trees and white sand in the bunkers.

🔢 D12 ✉ 5160 Las Vegas Boulevard ☎ 702/597-2400 🚍 Deuce; Strip trolley

BODY ENGLISH
www.hardrockhotel.com
Cavelike booths and innovative design create elegance with an edge at this buzzing two-tiered dance club. The energetic music avoids the endless techno drone.

🔢 F10 ✉ Hard Rock Hotel, 4455 Paradise Road ☎ 702/693-4000 🚍 108

CELEBRATION LOUNGE
www.tropicanalv.com
Entertaining singing bartenders offer up anything from Frank Sinatra to Patsy Cline and still find time to serve some of the best margaritas in the city.

🔢 D10 ✉ Tropicana, 3801 Las Vegas Boulevard South ☎ 702/739-2222 🎭 MGM Grand 🚍 Deuce; Strip trolley

COMEDY STOP
www.tropicanalv.com
Every night of the week you can laugh at three top comedians here, any one of whom you would go a long way to see. Ray Romano, Tim Allen and Drew Carey are just a few

of the well-known names who have taken to the stage at this venue.

🔢 D10 ✉ Tropicana, 3801 Las Vegas Boulevard South ☎ 702/739-2222 🎭 MGM Grand ⏰ Shows at 8pm and 10.30pm 🚍 Deuce; Strip trolley

COYOTE UGLY
www.nynyhotelcasino.com
If you enjoyed the movie or have visited the New York original, you'll love it here. It's a fun Southern-style saloon with wild bartenders who dance on the bar.

🔢 D10 ✉ New York–New York, 3790 Las Vegas Boulevard South ☎ 702/212-8804 🚍 Deuce; Strip trolley

TICKET INFORMATION
The popular long-running shows and the new ones sell out quickly, so it's advisable to make reservations. Call the relevant hotel or check out its website, which will have a reservation facility. Otherwise, shows can be reserved through TicketMaster (www.ticketmaster.com). Reservations are taken for long-running shows up to 30 days in advance; limited-time concerts or sporting events such as boxing matches can be reserved three months in advance. Note that shows can close with little notice so it is always best to check to avoid disappointment.

GRAND GARDEN ARENA
www.mgmgrand.com
This is one of the biggest venues in town, hosting huge events ranging from top entertainers to world championship boxing.

🔢 D10 ✉ MGM Grand, 3799 Las Vegas Boulevard South ☎ 702/891-7777 🎭 MGM Grand 🚍 Deuce; Strip trolley

HOLLYWOOD THEATER
www.mgmgrand.com
MGM's smaller venue hosting world-class performers–including Tom Jones and David Copperfield—also puts on top-line comedy acts.

🔢 D10 ✉ MGM Grand, 3799 Las Vegas Boulevard South ☎ 702/891-7777 🎭 MGM Grand 🚍 Deuce; Strip trolley

HOUSE OF BLUES
www.mandalaybay.com
Bringing New Orleans to Las Vegas, this superb, 1,500-seat venue is on three levels and features such big-name stars as B. B. King and Brian Ferry. There's great food, including the popular Sunday Gospel Brunch. Check out the unusual artworks, too.

🔢 D11 ✉ Mandalay Bay, 3950 Las Vegas Boulevard South ☎ 702/632-7600 🚍 Deuce; Strip trolley

IMAX MOVIE THEATER
www.luxor.com
The IMAX theater shows four 2-D and 3-D films a

day on a screen that is seven stories high. Or experience three motion simulator rides that take you to places you have never been before in ways you've never seen.

➕ D11 ✉ Luxor, 3900 Las Vegas Boulevard South
☎ 702/262-IMAX ⏰ Usually on the hour Sun–Thu 9am–11pm, Fri–Sat 9am–midnight
🚌 Deuce; Strip trolley

THE JOINT
www.hardrockhotel.com
One of Vegas' hottest venues, with a capacity of 1,400, the Joint brings in cutting-edge bands that are worthy of the Hard Rock image.

➕ F10 ✉ Hard Rock Hotel, 4455 Paradise Road
☎ 702/693-4000 🚌 108

MANDALAY BAY EVENTS CENTER
www.mandalaybay.com
This major venue hosts big-name concerts and sporting events. On one night, usually in June, it is transformed into a gigantic nightclub for the "Summer of Love" event.

➕ D11 ✉ Mandalay Bay, 3950 Las Vegas Boulevard South ☎ 702/632-7777
🚌 Deuce; Strip trolley

MONTE CARLO PUB AND BREWERY
www.montecarlo.com
Huge copper barrels enhance the rustic decor in this brewpub, where you can enjoy brick-oven pizzas, sandwiches, salads and platters…and, of

course, the beer that is brewed on the premises.

➕ D10 ✉ Monte Carlo, 3770 Las Vegas Boulevard South ☎ 702/730-7777
⏰ Mon–Thu 11am–2am, Fri 11am–4am, Sat 10am–4am, Sun 10am–2am 🚌 Deuce; Strip trolley

RA
www.ralv.com
House music, top DJs and go-go dancers set the scene at this chic Egyptian-theme club. On Wednesday is the "X-treme house party."

DRESS CODES

Most, if not all, of the nightclubs listed here impose quite a strict dress code, so it's a good idea to check what is acceptable beforehand. Men will have more trouble than women when it comes to what they are wearing: Jeans and sneakers are guaranteed to keep hopefuls out of any club. Women are also more likely than men to get in when there are long lines. You can get onto the VIP list if you know someone who works at the club, or if you have spent a lot in the casino. Otherwise, join the line outside the door (about an hour before opening time at the most popular places) and hope for the best. Cover charges, where they exist, are usually less than $20, and may be at different rates for men and women.

➕ D11 ✉ Luxor, 3900 Las Vegas Boulevard South
☎ 702/262-4949 🚌 Deuce; Strip trolley

RUMJUNGLE
www.mandalaybay.com
This sizzling hot club has a Caribbean theme and some breathtaking features—acrobats in harnesses launch themselves across the ceiling and there is a wall of flames and a waterfall.

➕ D11 ✉ Mandalay Bay, 3950 Las Vegas Boulevard South ☎ 702/632-7408
🚌 Deuce; Strip trolley

STUDIO 54
www.mgmgrand.com
Celebrities come to this high-energy club, a replica of the famous 1970s original in New York.

➕ D10 ✉ MGM Grand, 3799 Las Vegas Boulevard South ☎ 702/891-7254
🚇 MGM Grand 🚌 Deuce; Strip trolley

THOMAS & MACK CENTER/SAM BOYD STADIUM
www.thomasmack.com
State-of-the-art, multi-purpose arena that stages world-class entertainment and major national sports events, with a seating capacity of 19,511. From monster truck racing, boxing and show jumping to music concerts, rodeo, basketball and ice shows.

➕ G10 ✉ University of Nevada, South Maryland Parkway ☎ 702/895-3761
🚌 109

Restaurants

PRICES

Prices are approximate, based on a 3-course meal for one person.
$$$ over $50
$$ $20–$50
$ under $20

AUREOLE ($$$)

www.mandalaybay.com
This restaurant has big windows, glass-covered waterfalls and a massive award-winning wine tower. American dishes dominate the first-class menu here.

✚ D11 ✉ Mandalay Bay, 3950 Las Vegas Boulevard South ☎ 702/632-7447 ⏰ Daily 6–10.30 🚋 Deuce; Strip trolley

BAY SIDE ($$)

www.mandalaybay.com
Floor-to-ceiling windows here give sweeping views of the tropical lagoon outside. Although the buffet is not over-large, the cuisine is very good, with excellent salads, hearty meats and one of the better dessert selections, all made on the premises.

✚ D11 ✉ Mandalay Bay, 3950 Las Vegas Boulevard South ☎ 702/632-7447 ⏰ Daily 7am–10pm 🚋 Deuce; Strip trolley

BORDER GRILL ($$)

www.mandalaybay.com
Great Mexican home cooking in a lively setting. Lunch on spicy baby back ribs on the patio or get a take-out taco.

✚ D11 ✉ Mandalay Bay, 3950 Las Vegas Boulevard South ☎ 702/632-7447 ⏰ Sun–Thu 11.30–10.30, Fri, Sat 11.30–11 🚋 Deuce; Strip trolley

CHARLIE PALMER STEAK ($$$)

www.fourseasons.com/lasvegas
Subdued gleaming wood-work and bronze, and an exclusive atmosphere, set the scene for a meal that might include charcoal-grilled filet mignon or steamed halibut.

✚ D11 ✉ Four Seasons, 3960 Las Vegas Boulevard South ☎ 702/632-5000 ⏰ Daily 5.30–10.15 🚋 Deuce; Strip trolley

CHINA GRILL ($$$)

www.mandalaybay.com
Come with a group of friends or family and prepare to splurge on the massive portions in

A NEW IMAGE

Until recently, the only culinary experience for which Las Vegas was famous was the opportunity to stuff yourself with as much food as you could for a very reasonable price. Now the city has become renowned for the amount of choice available, with every kind of cuisine and style to suit every budget. For special-occasion dining in sumptuous surroundings, the best hotel restaurants are at the Bellagio, Mandalay Bay and the Venetian.

this imaginative Asian restaurant. Food is cooked in woks or under the grill—fish may be served whole, including the head.

✚ D11 ✉ Mandalay Bay, 3950 Las Vegas Boulevard South ☎ 702/632-7447 ⏰ Sun–Thu 5–11, Fri, Sat 5–midnight 🚋 Deuce; Strip trolley

CHOCOLATE SWAN ($$)

www.mandalaybay.com
This family-owned bakery and chocolate shop showcases creations made on-site. Enjoy wonderful desserts, made with the finest ingredients, either on the lovely patio or comfy sofas.

✚ D11 ✉ Mandalay Bay, 3950 Las Vegas Boulevard South ☎ 702/632-6753 ⏰ Daily 8am–10pm

EMERIL'S ($$$)

www.mgmgrand.com
This is a re-creation of Emeril Lagasse's popular, sophisticated New Orleans restaurant. The menu includes barbecued shrimp, veal sirloin, garlic pork chop and sumptuous banana cream pie.

✚ D10 ✉ MGM Grand, 3799 Las Vegas Boulevard South ☎ 702/891-7374 ⏰ Daily 11–2.30, 5.30–10.30 🚇 MGM Grand 🚋 Deuce; Strip trolley

FUSIA ($$$)

www.luxor.com
Fans of Asian cuisine will

love this stylish restaurant where familiar flavors are served with an exotic twist.
🔼 D11 ✉ Luxor, 3900 Las Vegas Boulevard South ☎ 702/262-4778 🕐 Sun–Thu 6–10.30, Fri, Sat 6–11 🚌 Deuce; Strip trolley

IL FORNAIO PANETTERIA ($)
www.nynyhotelcasino.com
It's worth making a special journey to this bakery café just for its espresso-mocha scone with chocolate chunks.
🔼 D10 ✉ New York–New York, 3790 Las Vegas Boulevard South ☎ 702/740-6969 🕐 Daily 7–9 🚇 MGM Grand 🚌 Deuce; Strip trolley

NOBHILL ($$$)
www.mgmgrand.com
A taste of San Francisco is brought to Vegas by celebrity chef Michael Mina. Finishing touches include five kinds of whipped potatoes to go with your tapioca-crusted rock cod, lobster pot pie or beef Wellington.
🔼 D10 ✉ MGM Grand, 3767 Las Vegas Boulevard South ☎ 702/891-7337 🕐 Sun–Thu 5–10, Fri, Sat 5–10.30 🚇 MGM Grand 🚌 Deuce; Strip trolley

NOODLE SHOP ($)
www.mandalaybay.com
The food here really hits the spot when you need sustenance in the early hours—or at any time of the day or night. It offers more than 20 kinds of noodle-and-rice dishes,

served hot and at lightning speed, plus barbecued meat dishes.
🔼 D11 ✉ Mandalay Bay, 3950 Las Vegas Boulevard South ☎ 702/632-7447 🕐 Daily 24 hours 🚌 Deuce; Strip trolley

PIETRO'S ($)
www.tropicanalv.com
An elegant and intimate place serving classic continental cuisine. Maître d', Pietro Musetto, ensures wonderful service and an unforgettable experience.
🔼 D10 ✉ Tropicana, 3801 Las Vegas Boulevard South ☎ 702/739-3561 🕐 Wed–Sun 5–11 🚇 MGM Grand 🚌 Deuce; Strip trolley

CHILD-FRIENDLY
Apart from the countless fast-food establishments selling hot dogs, burgers and pizzas, Las Vegas has many more options to prevent your kids from going hungry. Buffets enable them to pick and choose what they like, and most have an ice-cream machine that you can use to blackmail them into eating their greens. Theme restaurants that children will love include the Rainforest Café at the MGM Grand (✉ 3799 Las Vegas Boulevard South ☎ 702/891-8580; www. rainforestcafe.com 🕐 Sun–Thu 8am–11pm, Fri, Sat 8am–midnight), with jungle foliage, waterfalls, robotic animals and thunderstorms.

RED SQUARE ($$)
www.mandalaybay.com
Wash *latkes* and blinis down with vodka, or choose US and French dishes, in this Russian-theme restaurant where the headless statue of Lenin, the red-velvet drapes and the fake Communist propaganda give the game away.
🔼 D11 ✉ Mandalay Bay, 3950 Las Vegas Boulevard South ☎ 702/632-7407 🕐 Daily 5.30–midnight 🚌 Deuce; Strip trolley

TOTO'S ($)
This family-run restaurant serves enormous helpings of good Mexican food. It's popular with locals who welcome the good value.
🔼 H10 ✉ 2055 East Tropicana Avenue ☎ 702/895-7923 🕐 Mon–Sat 10–11, Sun 9.30–10 🚌 201

VERANDAH HIGH TEA ($$)
www.fourseasons.com/lasvegas
It's quite a surprise to find that great British institution, the afternoon tea, in the middle of Las Vegas. There are dainty sandwiches, scones with cream and jam, and French pastries, plus a selection of fine teas. Piano music completes the elegant scene. Reservations required.
🔼 D11 ✉ Four Seasons, 3960 Las Vegas Boulevard South ☎ 702/632-5000 🕐 Mon–Thu 3–4pm 🚌 Deuce; Strip trolley

With no less than seven theme hotels, this section of the Strip is capable of transporting you into a world of make-believe, with fire-spewing volcanoes and magical fountains.

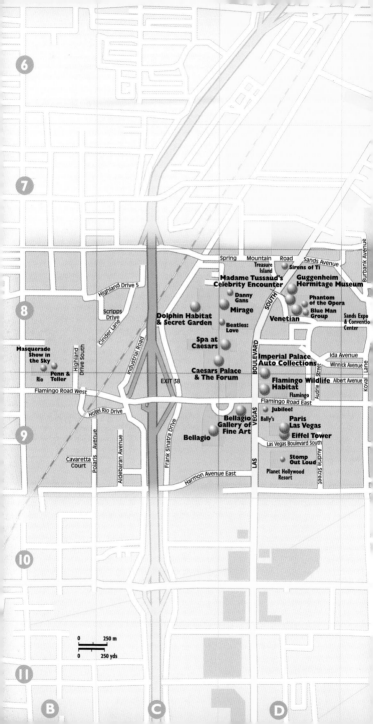

6

7

8

9

10

11

Spring Mountain Road

Sands Avenue

Treasure Island

Sirens of Ti

Madame Tussaud's
Celebrity Encounter

Guggenheim
Hermitage Museum

Danny
Gans

Phantom
of the Opera

Mirage

SOUTH

Blue Man
Group

Dolphin Habitat
& Secret Garden

Venetian

Sands Expo
& Convention
Center

Beatles:
Love

Spa at
Caesars

BOULEVARD

Imperial Palace
Auto Collections

Ida Avenue

Winnick Avenue

Masquerade
Show in
the Sky

Caesars Palace
& The Forum

Flamingo Wildlife
Habitat

Albert Avenue

Rio

Penn &
Teller

EXIT 38

Flamingo

Flamingo Road East

Flamingo Road West

Hotel Rio Drive

Jubilee!

Bally's

Paris
Las Vegas

Bellagio
Gallery of
Fine Art

VEGAS

Eiffel Tower

Las Vegas Boulevard South

Bellagio

LAS

Stomp
Out Loud

Cavaretta
Court

Planet Hollywood
Resort

Harmon Avenue East

Highland Drive S

Scripps
Drive

Cinder Lane

Highland
Drive South

Industrial Road

Frank Sinatra Drive

Polaris Avenue

Aldebaran Avenue

Burbank Avenue

Koval Lane

Audrie Street

Audrie Street

0   250 m

0   250 yds

B   **C**   **D**

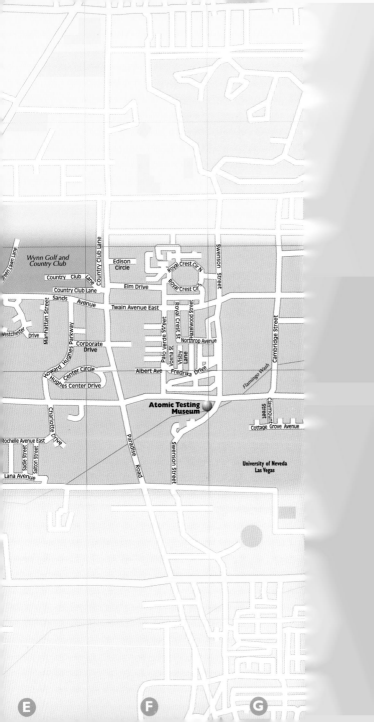

Bellagio

Showtime at Bellagio (left); a Chinese dragon greets guests (middle); the hotel pool (right)

THE BASICS

www.bellagio.com
✚ C9–D9
✉ 3600 Las Vegas Boulevard South
☎ 702/693-7111
🕐 Fountains: Mon–Fri 3pm–midnight, Sat, Sun 12–12; every half-hour to 8pm then every 15 mins (dependent on weather conditions)
🍴 Several cafés and restaurants
🚇 Bally's/Paris
🚌 Deuce; Strip trolley
💵 Fountains free
❓ No under-18s are allowed in Bellagio unless accompanied by a registered guest

HIGHLIGHTS

● Fountain show
● Gallery of Fine Art
● Botanical garden
● The lobby

The Italianate image for this $1.6 billion hotel, deemed to be one of the most opulent resorts in the world, was inspired by the village of Bellagio on the shores of Italy's Lake Como.

A touch of class A 10-acre (4ha) man-made lake at the front of the hotel sets the stage for the elegance, art and grandeur that awaits you inside. The dazzling front lobby has an 18ft (5.5m) ceiling with a chandelier of glass flowers suspended in the middle, designed by glass sculptor Dale Chihuly. All this splendor is enhanced by the wonderful botanical garden, set under a glass atrium.

Fountains at the Bellagio During the choreographed, computer-controlled fountain show, millions of gallons of water are sprayed to heights of 240ft (73m) above the hotel's massive lake. The system uses individually programmed water jets and atomizing nozzles that create an atmospheric fog on the lake; some jets can change the direction of the water, giving a dancing effect. The show is further enhanced by the integrated illumination that comes into play after dark, and by the audio system, with music ranging from Pavarotti to Sinatra.

So much The hotel's casino oozes sophistication, its slot machines encased in marble and wood. The Bellagio is proud of its Gallery of Fine Art (▷ 59), and its magnificent theater was styled after the Paris Opera specifically for Cirque du Soleil's "O" (▷ 65). The extravagant glass-enclosed shopping mall (▷ 64) has an array of exclusive boutiques.

Caesars Palace and the Forum

Hail Caesars, in all its glory (left); the Forum, famous for its incredible fountains (right)

So you're in Las Vegas, and the thing you most want to do is spend a day shopping for Italian-designer chic surrounded by the historic buildings of ancient Rome? No problem. It's all here at Caesars Palace.

Classical architecture Visit this superb complex and you could easily believe yourself transported into the Italian capital, amid architecture that spans the period from 300BC to AD1700. The grounds are filled with reproductions of Roman statues, marble columns and colonnades, and toga-clad cocktail waitresses and costumed centurions tend to your every need in the exciting casino.

Short days At the heart of things is the phenomenal shopping concourse, the Forum. Wander in and out of such stores as Versace and Armani, with an artificial sky overhead that gives the illusion that 24 hours have passed in just one hour. And when fatigue sets in, there's a big selection of restaurants.

Daily shows Every hour the Festival of Fountains springs into action, when statues come to life, special effects kick in, and you are entertained by characters from Roman mythology. In the Roman Great Hall, more special effects, animatronics, fire, water and smoke combine to portray the struggle to rule Atlantis, with the backdrop of a massive marine aquarium. The 4,000-seat Colosseum has hosted big-name shows, including Céline Dion and Elton John. Other attractions include a 3-D IMAX motion simulator where three-dimensional images and sound systems offer a unique experience.

THE BASICS

www.caesarspalace.com

✚ C8–D8

✉ 3570 Las Vegas Boulevard South

☎ 702/731-7110. The Forum/Race for Atlantis: 702/893-4800

🕐 Festival of Fountains/ Fall of Atlantis: Sun–Thu 10–10, Fri, Sat 10–11

🍴 Several cafés and restaurants

🚈 Flamingo/Caesars

🚌 Deuce; Strip trolley

♿ Festival of Fountains/ Fall of Atlantis: free

HIGHLIGHTS

● Marine aquarium
● Shops in the Forum
● Festival of Fountains
● Marble statuary and fountains

Dolphin Habitat and the Secret Garden

Here you can be entertained by marine mammals playing in their natural environment or get close up with some of the rarest and most exotic animals in the world, all in one afternoon.

Dolphins at play To the rear of the Mirage, the Dolphin Habitat's intent is to provide a happy and nurturing environment for Atlantic bottlenose dolphins and increase public awareness and the commitment to protect and conserve marine animals in general. Watch these amazing mammals frolic across a shimmering lagoon or below from the viewing gallery, and learn more about marine mammals on a 15-minute tour. The dolphins breed regularly, so you might be fortunate enough to see a baby at play. All the dolphins have names and respond to their keepers' instructions.

The dolphins come out to play; you can see Siegfried and Roy's white tigers in their habitat inside the Mirage at the south entrance (below left); Siegfried, Roy and a feline friend portrayed in bronze (bottom right)

Secret Garden Next to the Dolphin Habitat, Siegfried and Roy's Secret Garden re-creates a comfortable and secure jungle haven for five rare breeds of big cats: white lions of Timbavati, heterozygous Bengal tigers (possessing both tawny and white genes), the royal white tigers of Nevada, a panther and a snow leopard. An Asian elephant named Gildah, now in her mid-50s, holds a special place in everyone's heart. Observe these rare creatures as they live and play with only chain-link fences separating you from the animals.

Siegfried and Roy Illusionists Siegfried and Roy and their majestic tigers have enthralled crowds with their stage show at the Mirage since 1989. Unfortunately the performers' show was suspended in 2003 after Roy was mauled by one of their cats.

THE BASICS

www.miragehabitat.com

✚ C8

✉ The Mirage, 3400 Las Vegas Boulevard South

☎ 702/791-7188

🕐 Mon–Fri 11–5.30, Sat, Sun 10–5.30 (longer hours in summer); last admission 30 min before closing

🍴 Several cafés and restaurants at the Mirage

🚌 Deuce; Strip trolley

♿ Moderate

Guggenheim Hermitage Museum

A serious gallery space—the collection is strikingly set off against the dark walls

THE BASICS

www.guggenheim
lasvegas.org

➕ D8

✉ The Venetian, 3355 Las Vegas Boulevard South

☎ 702/414-2440

🕐 Daily 9.30–7.30

🍴 Several cafés and restaurants at the Venetian

🚌 Deuce; Strip trolley

♿ Moderate

DID YOU KNOW?

● There are four more Guggenheim museums in the world in addition to this one in Las Vegas, all part of the Guggenheim Foundation.

● The New York museum opened in 1959, while the Venice collection was donated by Peggy Guggenheim and opened in 1951. The spectacular Bilbao gallery in Spain and the Deutsche Guggenheim in Berlin, a joint venture between the bank and the museum, both opened their doors in 1997.

When the Guggenheim Hermitage Museum opened in September 2001 it added a new dimension to Las Vegas, an outstanding cultural institution that would offer stimulating art exhibitions to a new breed of tourist.

Dignified approach It would have been easy for the Venetian to continue its theme of replicating Venice with a re-creation of the Guggenheim's canalside modern art gallery in that city. Happily, they have instead created a serious art space, designed by architect Rem Koolhaas, in which to display the Guggenheim Foundation's wonderful collection, including classic works from Russia's State Hermitage Museum in St. Petersburg. These are set off against the dark, textured walls, within a free-standing structure inside the hotel.

The collection Solomon R. Guggenheim had a mission to educate the public about the type of art that drew upon pure artistic invention, and set about putting examples of abstract art on public display. The Guggenheim Foundation's extensive collection is based around this nonobjective form, but contains examples of all kinds of modern art, spanning the late 19th century to the present day, and including impressionism and abstract expressionism. It contains works by all the major artists who have played a significant role in the development of artistic style, and is particularly strong on postwar contemporary art. The Hermitage Museum in Las Vegas is most definitely on a par with New York's Metropolitan Museum of Art.

Imperial Palace Auto Collections

Dazzling examples at one of the largest showrooms in the world

The fifth level of the Imperial Palace parking facility takes on a rather different look from the other floors—this luxurious space displays a stunning collection of classic and special-interest cars, spanning a century of motoring.

Plush parking You could easily spend hours here, in what is one of the finest and largest automobile showrooms in the world. When it opened in 1981 the collection had 200 vehicles; since then, this number has increased to an impressive 750, although only 250 are displayed at one time. There are gleaming examples of all those classics that generations of drivers have yearned for, there are rare and exclusive models, and there are cars that represent landmarks in vehicle construction and technology. A significant acquisition for the exhibition here is the world's largest collection of Model J. Duesenbergs.

Famous and infamous owners Some of the vehicles that hold the greatest fascination are those that are noteworthy because of the people who drove them. You might see Marilyn Monroe's pink 1955 Lincoln Capri convertible, an armor-plated 1939 Mercedes-Benz used by Adolph Hitler, and cars owned by Al Capone, Elvis Presley, Benito Mussolini and James Cagney. There's no certainty about what will be on show because this is not exactly a straightforward museum, and the collection is not necessarily a permanent one. All of the exhibits are for sale, and serious buyers may well be among your fellow browsers on the lot.

THE BASICS

www.autocollections.com

⊞ D8–D9

✉ Imperial Palace, 3535 Las Vegas Boulevard South

☎ 702/794-3174

🕐 Daily 9.30–9.30

🍴 Several cafés and restaurants at the Imperial Palace

🚇 Harrah's/Imperial Palace

🚌 Deuce; Strip trolley

💵 Inexpensive

❓ Gift shop

DID YOU KNOW?

● Because of his germ phobia, Howard Hughes installed an air-purification system into his 1954 Chrysler that cost more than the car.
● President Truman's 1950 Lincoln Cosmopolitan had a gold-plated interior.
● The 1933 Silver Arrow displayed at the museum is one of only three still in existence today.

Madame Tussaud's

Enter the gateway to the stars and hang out with the celebs—even if they are made of wax

THE BASICS

www.mtvegas.com
🔲 D8
✉ The Venetian, 3377 Las Vegas Boulevard South
☎ 702/862-7800
🕐 Daily 10–10 (hours vary seasonally)
🍴 Several cafés and restaurants at the Venetian
🚌 Deuce; Strip trolley
💳 Expensive

HIGHLIGHTS

● "The King in Concert"
● "Marry Clooney"
● Behind-the-scenes tour

It is fitting that Madame Tussaud's first foray into the United States should be in Las Vegas, a magnet for both the biggest showbiz personalities and the most ardent celebrity-spotters.

Making an impression Madame Tussaud's is the world leader when it comes to making realistic likenesses in wax of the rich, famous and infamous. The secret is that they take an impression from the real person, rather than simply use an artist's sculpture, so every detail is absolutely spot on. Though this can be a rather claustrophobic experience (Napoleon was famously freaked out by it), celebrities regard it as at least one of the signs that they have made it in the business.

Las Vegas legends Not surprisingly, pride of place here goes to the superstars who have made their mark in Vegas—Wayne Newton, Tony Bennett, Engelbert Humperdinck, Tom Jones and the Rat Pack, to name just a few. Among more than 100 other masterfully produced figures is an international cast of movie and TV stars, icons from the music world and sport's big achievers.

Interactive experience Some exhibits allow you to interact with the famous models by taking part in a scenario, such as stepping into the hull of the *Black Pearl* to meet Disney's Captain Jack Sparrow. The highlight for every female must be the "Marry Clooney" exhibit, where you put on a wedding gown and walk down the aisle with George himself—in your dreams!

A taste of chic Paris, from fountain-splashed squares and the Eiffel Tower to the casino bar

Paris Las Vegas

Striving to capture the Parisian style of the most elegant of European cities, this hotel has succeeded in creating fine likenesses of the Eiffel Tower, Arc de Triomphe, Paris Opera House and the Louvre.

Joie de vivre This eye-catching resort may not be the real thing, but a characteristic exuberance is reflected in little touches like singing breadmen on bikes dressed in striped shirts and berets, and a joyful "Bonjour!" from roving street performers.

Eiffel Tower Experience The symbol of this hotel is the 525ft (160m) Eiffel Tower (half the size of the original), which was re-created using Gustav Eiffel's blueprints. A glass elevator takes you to the observation deck on the 50th floor for spectacular views of Las Vegas and the surrounding mountains—especially impressive at dusk when the Strip lights up. Eleven floors above the Strip is the sophisticated and pricey Eiffel Tower restaurant and bar.

Le Boulevard Don't miss this French-style shopping boulevard, which gives you a taste of one of Europe's most lively cities. Amid winding alleyways and cobbled streets, the ornate facades conceal elegant French boutiques, shops and restaurants. Weathered brickwork and brass lamps give an authentic rustic finish, and window boxes overflowing with bright blooms complete the Parisian picture. The very French Le Théâtre des Arts (▷ 65) plays host to the not-so-very-French Mel Brooks comedy stage show, *The Producers*.

THE BASICS

www.parislasvegas.com
✚ D9
✉ 3655 Las Vegas Boulevard South
☎ 702/946-7000
🕐 Eiffel Tower Experience: daily 10am–1am (weather permitting)
🍴 Several cafés and restaurants
Ⓑ Bally's/Paris
🚌 Deuce; Strip trolley
♿ Eiffel Tower Experience: moderate

HIGHLIGHTS

● Views from the observation deck of the Eiffel Tower
● Shopping at Le Boulevard
● Seeing a performance of *The Producers* at Le Théâtre des Arts

The Mirage

TOP 25

HIGHLIGHTS

● Volcanic eruption
● Secret Garden and white tigers
● Dolphin Habitat

TIP

● Note that the volcano eruption will be cancelled during bad weather or high winds.

There is nothing so fascinating as the power of nature, and to watch the Mirage's simulated volcano erupt or come face-to-face with the magnificent wildlife is a highlight that will enhance anyone's day.

Tropical delights This Polynesian-style resort is appropriately fronted by cascading waterfalls, tropical foliage and an imitation volcano. As you enter the lobby you can't miss the huge coral-reef aquarium stocked with tropical fish, and if you venture farther in you will discover a lush rain forest under a large atrium.

Eruptions to order You can wait years for a real volcano to create its spectacle, but here, in front of the Mirage, you can set your watch by it. The

Where there's smoke there's fire, and these are real flames erupting from the Mirage's volcano (left); one of the hotel's chic dining rooms (bottom left); The Mirage in neons (bottom right); a lush rain forest in the hotel atrium (below)

spectacular two-minute shows start with a rumbling sound, then a fog swirls around and a column of smoke and fire shoots 100ft (30m) into the sky. The computer-controlled show includes 34 gas-fueled special effects, with real flames on the water of the lagoon, and state-of-the-art lighting techniques. Arrive in good time so you can stake out a front-row position.

Wonderful wildlife Out the back of the Mirage is the Dolphin Habitat and Siegfried and Roy's Secret Garden (▷ 48–49). You can also see Siegfried and Roy's royal white tigers in the open-air white tiger habitat inside the Mirage at the south entrance, which is available for public viewing throughout the day and evening. These majestic animals laze around in a tropical atmosphere modeled on their natural habitat.

THE BASICS

www.themirage.com
✚ C8–D8
✉ 3400 Las Vegas Boulevard South
☎ 702/791-7111
🕐 Volcanic eruption: dusk–midnight on the hour
🍴 Several cafés and restaurants
🚌 Deuce; Strip trolley
🌋 Volcanic eruption: free

The Venetian

HIGHLIGHTS

- St. Mark's Square
- Grand Canal
- Guggenheim Hermitage Museum
- Grand Canal Shoppes
- Madame Tussaud's Celebrity Encounter

TIPS

- Reservations for gondola rides must be made in person on the same day.
- You will have to walk a lot to see the whole complex; wear comfortable shoes.

Owner Sheldon Adelson's replica of Venice has gone a long way to catch the flavor of this most romantic city. But at the same time it has retained all the glitz and pizzazz expected from Las Vegas.

Most authentic This $1.5 billion resort is one of the city's most aesthetically pleasing properties. The ornate lobby has domed and vaulted ceilings, exquisite marble floors and reproductions of frescoes framed in gold. An excellent take on Venice, it has its own 1,200ft-long (365m) Grand Canal—the real one extends 2.5 miles (4km). The waterway meanders under arched bridges, including the Rialto, and past the vibrant piazza of St. Mark's Square and other familiar Venice landmarks. In the casino hang the replica works of artists Tiepolo, Tintoretto and Titian. The Venetian is also home to

The stunning opulence of the Venetian's lobby (left); masterpieces adorn the casino ceiling (right); the Grand Canal (bottom left) and St. Mark's campanile (top middle) re-created on the Strip; get in the swim of things at the pool complex (bottom middle); a singing gondolier takes guests on a musical journey (bottom right)

Madame Tussaud's (▷ 52) interactive wax museum and the Guggenheim Hermitage Museum (▷ 50).

Gondola ride From St. Mark's you can board a gondola and be carried down the Grand Canal to the soothing sound of water lapping against the sides; there is even a wedding gondola if you want to take the plunge. Everything looks particularly spectacular at dusk, when the spirit of Venice is really captured.

Time to shop The Grand Canal Shoppes mall lines an indoor cobblestoned plaza alongside the canal and is linked by walkways. There are fine restaurants and interesting shops behind faux facades where strolling opera singers perform Italian arias and various other street entertainers do their thing.

THE BASICS

www.venetian.com
🔲 D8
✉ 3355 Las Vegas Boulevard South
☎ 702/414-3772. Grand Canal Shoppes/gondola ride: 702/414-4500
🕐 Gondola ride: Sun–Thu 10am–11pm, Fri, Sat 10am–midnight; last ride leaves 15 min before closing
🍽 Several cafés and restaurants
🚍 Deuce; Strip trolley
♿ Gondola ride: moderate

More to See

ATOMIC TESTING MUSEUM
www.atomictestingmuseum.org
Opened in February 2005, this is the first museum of its kind in the US and provides an interesting insight into the work of the Nevada Test Site and its impact. Three miles (5km) from the Strip, the museum is certainly something different and a long way from the superficial hype of Vegas. Interactive exhibits help you learn about the history of nuclear power.
✚ F9 ✉ 755 East Flamingo Road ☎ 702/794-5151 ⏱ Mon–Sat 9–5, Sun 1–5 🚌 202 💲 Moderate

THE BEATLES LOVE
www.thebeatleslove.com
The latest Cirque du Soleil production celebrates the musical legacy of The Beatles and explores their songs in a series of scenes inhabited by real and imaginary people. Staged in a purpose-built circular theater.
✚ D8 ✉ The Mirage, 3400 Las Vegas Boulevard South ☎ 702/792-7777 ⏱ Thu–Mon 7 and 10pm 🚌 Deuce; Strip trolley 💲 Very Expensive

BELLAGIO GALLERY OF FINE ART
www.bgfa.biz
The first gallery on the Strip, showing a serious side to Las Vegas culture. The facility is a noncommercial venue that showcases two high-quality art exhibitions per year from major museums across the US and beyond.
✚ D9 ✉ Bellagio, 3600 Las Vegas Boulevard South ☎ 702/693-7111 ⏱ Daily 9am–10pm; last admission 9.30pm 🚌 Deuce; Strip trolley 💲 Moderate

BLUE MAN GROUP
www.venetian.com
The most unusual show in Vegas—a group of guys with bright cobalt-blue bald heads, performing hilarious routines in which artistic canvases are created by the strangest means.
✚ D8 ✉ The Venetian, 3355 Las Vegas Boulevard South ☎ 702/414-1000 ⏱ Nightly 7.30 (also 10.30 Tue and Sat) 🚌 Deuce; Strip trolley 💲 Very expensive

DANNY GANS
www.themirage.com
Impressionist extraordinaire Danny

★

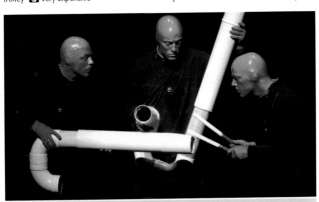

The weird and wonderful Blue Man Group

Gans blends song, dance, comedy and acting into a seamless stream of up to 100 different characters a night. ✚ D8 ✉ The Mirage, 3400 Las Vegas Boulevard South ☎ 702/792-7777 🕐 Tue, Wed, Fri, Sat 8pm 🚌 Deuce; Strip trolley ✋ Very expensive

FLAMINGO WILDLIFE HABITAT
www.flamingolasvegas.com
A lush 15-acre (6ha) paradise has been re-created at the Flamingo to provide a home to more than 300 exotic birds, including flamingos and penguins. Don't miss the penguin feeding times at 8.30am and 3pm. ✚ D9 ✉ Flamingo, 3555 Las Vegas Boulevard South ☎ 702/733-3111 🕐 Daily 24 hours 🚇 Flamingo/Caesars 🚌 Deuce; Strip trolley ✋ Free

JUBILEE!
www.ballyslasvegas.com
Jubilee's scantily clad showgirls in massive headdresses and little else—many appear topless—remain as popular as when the show opened in 1981. Though the original concept remains unchanged, brand-new routines and segments are introduced on a regular basis. ✚ D9 ✉ Bally's, 3645 Las Vegas Boulevard South ☎ 702/739-4111 🕐 Sat–Thu 7.30pm and 10.30pm 🚇 Bally's/Paris 🚌 Deuce; Strip trolley ✋ Very expensive ❓ Minimum age limit 18 years

MASQUERADE SHOW IN THE SKY
www.riolasvegas.com
It's carnival time every day at the Rio. Mardi Gras floats are suspended from the ceiling parade above the casino floor. ✚ B8 ✉ Rio, 3700 West Flamingo Road ☎ 702/777-7777 🕐 Shows at 3, 4, 5, 6.30, 7.30, 8.30, 9.30 🚌 202

PENN AND TELLER
www.riolasvegas.com
This talented partnership combines magic, illusions, juggling, comedy and stunts in an intelligent show. ✚ B8 ✉ Rio, 3700 West Flamingo Road ☎ 702/777-7777 🕐 Daily 9pm 🚌 202 ✋ Very expensive

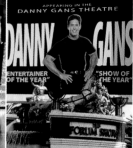

Bring on the dancing girls, Jubilee!

Impressionist Danny Gans at the Mirage

PHANTOM OF THE OPERA

www.phantomlasvegas.com
Andrew Lloyd Webber's musical
phenomenon opened in 2006 in the
majestic grandeur of the Venetian.
🚼 D8 ✉ The Venetian, 3355 Las Vegas
Boulevard South ☎ 702/414-7469
🕐 Wed–Mon 7pm and 10pm (hours can vary)
🚌 Deuce; Strip trolley 💰 Very expensive

SIRENS OF TI

www.treasureisland.com
A swashbuckling battle between sexy
sirens and renegade pirates that takes
place at Siren's Cove, at the hotel
entrance. There's music, seductive
dancing and plenty of explosions.
🚼 D8 ✉ Treasure Island, 3300 Las Vegas
Boulevard South ☎ 702/894-7111
🕐 Nightly 5.30, 7, 8.30, 10 (dependent on
weather); shows last 90 min 🚌 Deuce; Strip
trolley 💰 Free

SPA AT CAESARS PALACE

In addition to the first-class spa treatments and exercise equipment here,
there's a beautiful outdoor area,
where you can relax amid statues and
topiary beside three superb swimming
pools. Luxury poolside cabanas are for
rent, and come with waiter service,
TVs and massage service.
🚼 D8 ✉ Caesars Palace, 3570 Las Vegas
Boulevard South ☎ 702/731-7776 🕐 Daily
6am–8pm; hotel guests only on Fri and Sat
🚇 Flamingo/Caesars 🚌 Deuce; Strip trolley

STOMP OUT LOUD

www.planethollywoodresort.com
The international stage sensation
STOMP arrived at the Planet
Hollywood resort (formerly the
Aladdin) in April 2007. Performed in a
theater built especially for the show,
this version has been transformed for
Las Vegas in a way that has never
been seen before. The unique combi-
nation of percussion—using objects
such as brooms, boxes, drums and
garbage bins—dance, acrobatics and
comedy enthralls the audience from
start to finish.
🚼 D9 ✉ Planet Hollywood Resort, 3367
Las Vegas Boulevard South ☎ 702/785-
5555 🕐 Nightly 8pm 🚇 Bally's/Paris
🚌 Deuce; Strip trolley 💰 Expensive

Let battle commence, Sirens of Ti

Heart of the Strip

A walk through the heart of the Strip, stopping at some of the major resort hotels to experience a sample of what they have to offer.

DISTANCE: About 2 miles (3km) **ALLOW:** 3 hours

START

MIRACLE MILE
⊞ D9 🚌 Deuce; Strip trolley

END

THE VENETIAN
⊞ D8 🚌 Deuce; Strip trolley

1 Wander through the sparkling new Miracle Mile shopping mall (▷ 63). Stick around long enough to do a spot of window shopping and admire the sleek surroundings.

2 Back outside, walk north to Paris (▷ 53) and take the elevator to the top of the Eiffel Tower. Cross the boulevard to Bellagio (▷ 46), home to the ultimate water attraction.

3 From Bellagio, take the elevated walkway across Flamingo Road to Caesars Palace (▷ 47) for the Atlantis talking statue show.

4 Go left from Caesars Palace to The Mirage (▷ 54). Out the back you can watch the dolphins play for a while and then move on to see the big cats that live here.

8 Choose one of the many refreshment stops to recharge your batteries and then take a relaxing gondola ride to finish your walk.

7 Cross the footbridge over to the Venetian (▷ 56), where the cityscape of Venice has been replicated. Here you'll find a network of canals, lined by Venetian-style architecture and crossed by pretty little bridges where you can while away the time.

6 From the Mirage, walk north on the Strip until you get to the Treasure Island resort (if operating, hop on the tram if you want to take the strain off your feet). Try to time it right for the start of the Sirens of Ti show (▷ 61).

5 Retrace your steps back through the hotel. Note the aquarium in reception.

Shopping

BARNES & NOBLE

This is one of several Vegas branches of the colossally well-stocked general bookstore. It has impressive children's and best-seller sections.

🔲 G7 ✉ 3860 South Maryland Parkway ☎ 702/734-2900 🚌 109

CAROLINA HERRERA

Opened in 2004, this store is dedicated to Herrera's lifestyle collection for men and women. The range includes chic tailored suits, glam evening wear, cotton shirts and accessories.

🔲 D8 ✉ The Forum, 3570 Las Vegas Boulevard South ☎ 702/893-4800 🚌 Deuce; Strip trolley

CHIHULY STORE

This shop has a good representation of the respected glass sculptor's vibrant hand-blown pieces. It's fitting that Chihuly opened his first gallery here—his biggest sculpture hangs from the Bellagio's (▷ 46) lobby ceiling.

🔲 D9 ✉ Bellagio, 3600 Las Vegas Boulevard South ☎ 702/693-7995 🚌 Deuce; Strip trolley

FIELD OF DREAMS

This is the place for one-off sport and celebrity memorabilia, from items such as an electric guitar signed by musician Carlos Santana to a jersey autographed by football player Dan Marino.

🔲 B8 ✉ Masquerade Village, Rio, 3700 West Flamingo Road ☎ 702/777-7777 🚌 202

GIANNI VERSACE

The late designer's colorful Italian style is obvious in the garments sold here, all made from the finest fabrics. The company's signature lion's head appears on everything.

🔲 D8 ✉ The Forum, 3570 Las Vegas Boulevard South ☎ 702/893-4800 🚌 Deuce; Strip trolley

GRAND CANAL SHOPPES

This chic, Italian-theme mall stretches along a

replica of Venice's Grand Canal. Here you'll find over 75 of the most exclusive stores in the world, ranging from Davidoff cigars and Mikimoto (▷ below) pearls to Jimmy Choo shoes.

🔲 D8 ✉ The Venetian, 3355 Las Vegas Boulevard South ☎ 702/414-1000 🚌 Deuce; Strip trolley

MASQUERADE VILLAGE

Stroll down the tiled streets here to find quirky places such as the Nawlins Store, carrying voodoo supplies and good luck charms. Elsewhere in the mall, sportswear and memorabilia are on sale.

🔲 B8 ✉ Rio, 3700 West Flamingo Road ☎ 702/777-7777 🚌 202

MIKIMOTO

Exquisite Akoya cultured pearls and South Sea pearl jewelry are sold here among other gift items.

🔲 D8 ✉ Grand Canal Shoppes, 3355 Las Vegas Boulevard South ☎ 702/414-3900 🚌 Deuce; Strip trolley

MIRACLE MILE

A new name and new look for the Desert Passage shopping mall, with work scheduled to be completed by the end of 2007 as part of the Aladdin Hotel's multimillion transition into Planet Hollywood. Out goes the Moroccan theme and in comes a more

urbanized, sleeker feel. The mall will have 170 stores, 15 restaurants and live entertainment.
⊞ D8 🔲 3355 Las Vegas Boulevard South ☎ 702/737-3100 🚍 Deuce; Strip trolley

SHOWCASE SLOTS & ANTIQUES

This is a nostalgic collection of antique slot machines, early video poker machines, jukeboxes and neon signs.
⊞ D6 🔲 4305 South

Industrial Road ☎ 702/740-5722 🚍 203

VIA BELLAGIO

This opulent mall will tempt you with its exquisite fashion and jewelry collections from world-renowned designers Giorgio Armani, Chanel, Gucci, Prada, Tiffany & Co. and lots more.
⊞ C9 🔲 Bellagio, 3600 Las Vegas Boulevard South ☎ 702/693-7111 🚍 Deuce; Strip trolley

WINE CELLAR

An impressive selection of wines (more than 45,000 bottles) from the world's top viticulture regions. Prices range from reasonable to astronomical for some of the rare vintages, such as the 1855 to 1990 vertical collection of Chateau d'Yquem, valued at $2 million. Wine tastings.
⊞ B8 🔲 Rio, 3700 West Flamingo Road ☎ 702/777-7962 🚍 202

Entertainment and Nightlife

CLEOPATRA'S BARGE

www.caesarspalace.com
The name reveals the theme at this floating club—a replica of the vessel that carried Cleopatra along the Nile. During the week, a DJ plays contemporary dance music, and there's live music on weekends.
⊞ D8 🔲 Caesars Palace, 3570 Las Vegas Boulevard South ☎ 702/731-7110 🚍 Deuce; Strip trolley

COLOSSEUM

www.caesarspalace.com
A magnificent auditorium purpose-built for Céline Dion's extravaganza that came to a close in 2007.
⊞ D8 🔲 Caesars Palace, 3570 Las Vegas Boulevard South ☎ 702/731-7110 📍 Flamingo/Caesars 🚍 Deuce; Strip trolley

EIFFEL TOWER BAR

www.parislasvegas.com
This sophisticated, elegant bar is inside the restaurant, 11 floors up. Stop by for a drink and take in the most stunning views of Las Vegas in all its glory.
⊞ D9 🔲 Paris Las Vegas, 3655 Las Vegas Boulevard South ☎ 702/948-6937 📍 Bally's/Paris 🚍 Deuce; Strip trolley

FLAMINGO SHOWROOM

www.flamingolasvegas.com
From the very beginning the Flamingo has hosted show business legends—Nat King Cole and Jerry Lewis have graced the stage here. Currently, singer Toni Braxton is appearing, plus top comedy group Second City.

⊞ D9 🔲 Flamingo, 3555 Las Vegas Boulevard South ☎ 702/733-3333 📍 Flamingo/Caesars 🚍 Deuce; Strip trolley

GHOST BAR

www.palms.com
One of Vegas's most talked about bars, with a simple, yet eclectic look, is atop the Palms Hotel. Marvel at the breathtaking views from 55 floors up while music from the DJ fills the background. From the outside deck is yet another fantastic view, one from a glass floor looking directly down at the Palms Pool below. A young and trendy crowd mix with the celebrity clientele.
⊞ A9 🔲 Palms, 4321 Flamingo Road ☎ 702/938-2666 🚍 202

GORDON-BIERSCH LAS VEGAS

Exposed pipes and gleaming brewing equipment set the stage for this hangout, popular with local yuppies. The beers include tasty German brews that are changed seasonally.
F7 ⊠ 3987 Paradise Road ☎ 702/312-5247 🚌 108

IMPROV COMEDY CLUB

www.harrahs.com
Two comedy shows a night (except Mon) feature emerging stars from a branch of the famous Improv comedy club.
D8 ⊠ Harrah's, 3475 Las Vegas Boulevard South ☎ 702/369-5111 🚇 Harrah's/Imperial Palace 🚌 Deuce; Strip trolley

JAPONAIS

www.themirage.com
Relax in this exotic lounge amid tropical foliage and lulled by the soothing sound of waterfalls.
D8 ⊠ The Mirage, 3400 Las Vegas Boulevard South ☎ 702/791-7111 🚌 Deuce; Strip trolley

MIST BAR

www.treasureisland.com
A lively crowd comes to this relaxed spot, with its neighborhood-bar atmosphere, to watch sports on large plasma screens and to listen to rock and pop.
D8 ⊠ Treasure Island, 3300 Las Vegas Boulevard South ☎ 702/894-7111 🚌 Deuce; Strip trolley

NAPOLEON'S

www.parislasvegas.com
The French theme here incorporates French wines and beers, and French-style hot and cold appetizers. Live jazz.
D9 ⊠ Paris Las Vegas, 3655 Las Vegas Boulevard South ☎ 702/946-6349 🚇 Bally's/Paris 🚌 Deuce; Strip trolley

RISQUÉ

www.parislasvegas.com
A sensual ultralounge attracting a sophisticated crowd with plush couches, velvet drapes, crystal chandeliers, mirrored lighting effects and a lit dance floor where music plays well into the night. Intimate balconies offer views over the Strip.
D9 ⊠ Paris Las Vegas, 3655 Las Vegas Boulevard

CIRQUE DU SOLEIL

This remarkable troupe that originated in Montréal has taken circus arts to unprecedented new levels with its breathtaking skills and supremely artistic concept shows. It has totally won over Las Vegas, with several shows currently running: **Mystère** at Treasure Island (Wed–Sun); **"O"** at Bellagio (Wed–Sun); **Zumanity** at New York-New York (Fri–Tue); **Kà** at MGM Grand (Tue–Sat); **The Beatles Love** at the Mirage (▷ 59). For further details www.cirquedusoleil.com

South ☎ 702/946-4589 🚇 Bally's/Paris 🚌 Deuce; Strip trolley

LE THEATRE DES ARTS

www.parislasvegas.com
Natalie Cole and Tony Bennett are among the artists who have appeared at this 1,200-seat theater, which is currently staging *The Producers*.
D9 ⊠ Paris Las Vegas, 3655 Las Vegas Boulevard South ☎ 702/946-7000 🚇 Bally's/Paris 🚌 Deuce; Strip trolley

UNLV PERFORMING ARTS CENTER

www.pac.unlv.edu
See major international artists perform classical and popular music, dance, theater, ballet and opera. The center comprises the Artemus W. Ham Concert Hall (home to the Nevada Symphony Orchestra), the Judy Bayley Theater and the Black Box Theater.
G9 ⊠ University of Nevada, 4505 South Maryland Parkway ☎ 702/895-2787 🚌 109

V BAR

www.venetian.com
Enclosed in opaque glass walls, this high-roller's joint oozes sophistication. Sleek lines, leather chaise longues and subdued lighting enhance the sultry atmosphere.
D8 ⊠ The Venetian, 3355 Las Vegas Boulevard South ☎ 702/414-3200 🚌 Deuce; Strip trolley

Restaurants

PRICES

Prices are approximate, based on a 3-course meal for one person.

$$$	over $50
$$	$20–$50
$	under $20

BATTISTA'S HOLE IN THE WALL ($$)

www.battistaslasvegas.com
For more than 30 years people have been flocking here for the excellent Italian food, served with style.

✚ D9 ✉ 4041 Audrie Street ☎ 702/732-1424 ⏰ Daily 5–10.30 🚋 Flamingo/Caesars 🚌 Deuce; Strip trolley

BELLAGIO BUFFET ($$)

More expensive than most buffets, this is probably the most highly regarded. It has many different types of cuisine, including Italian, Chinese and Japanese, in a European marketplace-style setting.

✚ C9 ✉ Bellagio, 3600 Las Vegas Boulevard South ☎ 702/693-7111 ⏰ Sun–Thu 8am–10pm, Fri, Sat 8am–11pm 🚌 Deuce; Strip trolley

BIG KITCHEN ($$)

www.ballyslasvegas.com
Looking for all the world just like a gigantic kitchen, this buffet offers excellent value and hardly any waiting time. An enormous selection of such comfort foods as fried chicken and meat loaf sits alongside more interesting seafood and Chinese specialties, and the portions are big.

✚ D9 ✉ Bally's, 3645 Las Vegas Boulevard South ☎ 702/967-7999 ⏰ Daily 7am–10pm 🚋 Bally's/Paris 🚌 Deuce; Strip trolley

BOUCHON ($$)

www.bouchonbistro.com
World-renowned chef Thomas Keller showcases his bistro fare that delights both the palate and the eye at Bouchon, located in the Venetian Tower. Deep blue velvet seating, antique lights, a mosaic floor and hand-painted murals provide a warm café-style ambience amid an enchanting poolside garden.

✚ D8 ✉ The Venetian 3355 Las Vegas Boulevard South

BUFFET KNOW-HOW

Buffets offer breakfast, lunch and dinner, with a different range of food available at each meal. They are a great option for families, particularly those that include fussy eaters, because there is sure to be something for everyone. Buffets also offer tremendous value for the money. This does, of course, mean that they are popular and lines can be long, especially at peak times–at the most popular buffets, it can take up to three hours to eat your meal.

☎ 702/414-6200 ⏰ Daily 7–10.30, 5–11, also Sat, Sun 11.30–2.30 🚌 Deuce; Strip trolley

BRADLEY OGDEN ($$$)

www.caesarspalace.com
This famed San Francisco chef has earned national acclaim for his classic, fresh American cooking. Polished floors and dark wood give a sleek look to the elegant and refined dining room where serious, quality food is served with a first-class professional service.

✚ D8 ✉ Caesars Palace, 3750 Las Vegas Boulevard South ☎ 702/731-7110 ⏰ Daily 5–11 🚋 Flamingo/Caesars 🚌 Deuce; Strip trolley

CANALETTO ($$$)

www.venetian.com
Where better to sample good northern Italian cuisine than on a re-creation of Venice's St. Mark's Square? Some little-known Italian wines are on offer, too.

✚ D8 ✉ The Venetian, 3355 Las Vegas Boulevard South ☎ 702/733-0070 ⏰ Mon–Fri 11.30–11, Sat, Sun 11.30–midnight 🚌 Deuce; Strip trolley

CARNIVAL WORLD ($$)

www.playrio.com
This is one of the best buffets in Las Vegas, with chefs cooking on view at various points around the serving islands. There are

11 styles of cuisine, from Brazilian to Mongolian.
🔳 B8 ✉ Rio, 3700 West Flamingo Road ☎ 702/777-7777 ◷ Mon–Fri 7–10, Sat, Sun 7.30–10 🚌 202

DRAI'S ($$$)

www.barbarycoastcasino.com
Come here for excellent French food, a contemporary setting and a divine chocolate mousse. Live jazz is played.
🔳 D9 ✉ Barbary Coast, 3595 Las Vegas Boulevard South ☎ 702/737-0555 ◷ Daily 5.30–midnight 🚌 Deuce; Strip trolley

FRANCESCO'S ($$)

www.treasureisland.com
Superb Italian fare is a real bonus at this friendly and relaxed restaurant—try the pancetta-wrapped scallops.
🔳 D8 ✉ Treasure Island, 3300 Las Vegas Boulevard South ☎ 702/894-7111 ◷ Daily 5–10.30 🚌 Deuce; Strip trolley

HARLEY DAVIDSON CAFÉ ($)

www.harley-davidsoncafe.com
Motorcycle buffs will enthuse over this American roadside café. Many gleaming machines are on display, including one owned by Elvis, and memorabilia covers the walls. Try the tollhouse-cookie pie.
🔳 D9 ✉ 3575 Las Vegas Boulevard South ☎ 702/740-4555 ◷ Sun–Thu 11–11, Fri, Sat 11am–midnight 🚌 Deuce; Strip trolley

HOUSE OF LORDS ($$)

www.saharavegas.com
Once the haunt of visiting stars, this comfortable restaurant remains popular for its traditional cuisine. Dishes include roasted crab cakes, prime rib and cherries jubilee.
🔳 F6 ✉ Sahara, 2535 Las Vegas Boulevard South ☎ 702/737-2111 ◷ Daily 5–10 🚌 Sahara 🚌 Deuce; Strip trolley

HYAKUMI ($$)

www.caesarspalace.com
This is another Japanese restaurant where teppanyaki chefs prepare your meal at your table with great flair and entertainment value. There's a

TASTE THE GOOD LIFE

In addition to the endless variety of eateries catering to visitors on a more restricted budget, a new type of restaurant has surfaced in Las Vegas. During the 1990s, fashionable eateries and stand-alone fine-dining establishments made their mark on the city. World-famous chefs with the best credentials—such as Puck, Lagasse, Palmer, Vongerichten, Mori, Sotelino and Matsuisa—were lured to Vegas to meet the demands of increasing numbers of sophisticated travelers visiting the city. As a result, food has evolved into another attraction with a Las Vegas flavor.

good range of sake, too.
🔳 D8 ✉ Caesars Palace, 3570 Las Vegas Boulevard South ☎ 702/731-7110 ◷ Daily 5–11 🚌 Flamingo/Caesars 🚌 Deuce; Strip trolley

KOKOMO'S ($$)

www.themirage.com
Tropical surroundings complement the delicious Hawaiian cuisine, including fish with broiled bananas and coconut shrimp.
🔳 D8 ✉ The Mirage, 3400 Las Vegas Boulevard South ☎ 702/791-7111 ◷ Daily 5–10.30 🚌 Deuce; Strip trolley

LAWRY'S THE PRIME RIB ($$$)

www.lawrysonline.com
Lawry's is popular for its perfectly cooked, tasty prime rib, which is carved at the table. Waitresses in stylish brown-and-white uniforms and starched white caps tend to your every need in the art deco surroundings.
🔳 E9 ✉ 4043 Howard Hughes Parkway ☎ 702/893-2223 ◷ Sun–Thu 5–10, Fri, Sat 5–11 🚌 202

MICHAEL MINA ($$$)

www.michaelmina.net
Enjoy seafood favorites that Chef Michael Mina has made famous with his daring approach, using unexpected flavors and textures blended with Mediterranean and Californian ingredients. Distinguished and sleek,

yet casual, this is the perfect place to try Mina's signature dishes.

🔡 C9 ⊠ Bellagio, 3600 Las Vegas Boulevard South ☎ 702/693-7223 ⓘ Daily 5.30–10 🚌 Deuce; Strip trolley

MON AMI GABI ($$)

www.parislasvegas.com
Enjoy fine French fare in the atrium here (with an open sunroof) or on the patio. Tables are set beneath sparkling white lights, from where you get a great view of the Bellagio's fountain show.

🔡 D9 ⊠ Paris Las Vegas, 3655 Las Vegas Boulevard South ☎ 702/944-4224 ⓘ Sun–Thu 11.30–1.30, 5–11, Fri, Sat 11.30–3.30, 5–midnight 🚇 Bally's/Paris 🚌 Deuce; Strip trolley

NERO'S ($$$)

www.caesarspalace.com
Maine lobster, swordfish and grilled ahi feature on the menu of this popular restaurant, along with hearty steaks.

🔡 D8 ⊠ Caesars Palace, 3570 Las Vegas Boulevard South ☎ 702/731-7110 ⓘ Daily 5–11 🚇 Flamingo/Caesars 🚌 Deuce; Strip trolley

PARADISE GARDEN BUFFET ($$)

www.flamingolasvegas.com
Enjoy the view of cascading waterfalls and wildlife through large picture windows while you dine on crab, shrimp, prime rib, large salads and

everything else in between. There's also a large dessert choice.

🔡 D9 ⊠ Flamingo, 3555 Las Vegas Boulevard ☎ 702/733-3333 ⓘ Daily 7–2.30, 4.30–10 🚇 Flamingo/Caesars 🚌 Deuce; Strip trolley

PICASSO ($$$)

www.bellagiolasvegas.com
This is among the best restaurants in Vegas, with refined cuisine reflecting places where the artist lived (south of France and Spain). And the Picasso paintings on the walls are authentic.

🔡 C9 ⊠ Bellagio, 3600 Las Vegas Boulevard South ☎ 702/693-7223 ⓘ Wed–Mon 6–9.30 🚌 Deuce; Strip trolley

POSTRIO ($$)

www.venetian.com
Enjoy Wolfgang Puck's American dishes in an elegant dining room or casual café on St. Mark's Square.

JUST DESSERTS

If it's dessert you're after, then pay a visit to Lenôtre in Le Boulevard at Paris Las Vegas (▷ 53) for a mouthwatering assortment of French pastries, éclairs and cookies that can be enjoyed in a café-style atmosphere. At the Venetian (▷ 56–57), Tintoretto's Bakery also has luscious homemade pastries and cookies.

🔡 D8 ⊠ The Venetian, 3355 Las Vegas Boulevard South ☎ 702/796-1110 ⓘ Sun–Thu 11.30–10, Fri, Sat 11.30–11 🚌 Deuce; Strip trolley

TILTED KILT ($)

www.playrio.com
This Irish-American pub serves hearty Irish food, and Irish beer and stout are on tap. There's also Irish music and memorabilia, plus darts.

🔡 B8 ⊠ Rio, 3700 West Flamingo Road ☎ 702/777-7777 ⓘ Mon–Fri 4pm–2am, Sat, Sun noon–2am 🚌 202

VALENTINO ($$$)

www.venetian.com
Linger over superb modern Italian cuisine in a remarkable setting at this top-class restaurant, owned by celebrity restaurateur Piero Selvaggio.

🔡 D8 ⊠ The Venetian, 3355 Las Vegas Boulevard South ☎ 702/414-3000 ⓘ Daily 11.30–11 🚌 Deuce; Strip trolley

VILLAGE SEAFOOD ($$)

www.playrio.com
Fish, fish and more fish— in fact, nothing but seafood is served here. Even so, there's plenty of choice, with dishes prepared in just about every way you could imagine.

🔡 B8 ⊠ Rio, 3700 West Flamingo Road ☎ 702/777-7777 ⓘ Sun–Thu 4–10, Sat, Sun 3–11 🚌 202

This stretch is a mixture of old and new. Steve Wynn's sparkling multimillion dollar hotel, Wynn Vegas, overshadows old faithfuls such as the Sahara and Circus Circus that were part of the Golden Era.

Circus Circus

HIGHLIGHTS

● The Canyon Blaster ride
● The Rim Runner ride
● The Chaos ride
● IMAX Cineplex
● Big Top circus acts

TIPS

● Height restrictions may apply on some rides.
● If you're intending to stay a while at the Adventuredome, the daily pass can save you money.

The circus has come to town. In fact, it arrived here on the Strip in 1968, when Circus Circus opened its doors to provide the city with its first gaming concern offering family entertainment.

Roll up, roll up At first there were no hotel rooms at Circus Circus, only a casino and the world's biggest permanent circus tent. Today, however, around 1,500 guest rooms are stacked in towers behind the first-floor casino, while the upper floor has a wealth of carnival attractions and arcade games surrounding a circus arena. Acrobats, trapeze artists, aerialists and clowns are just some of the acts that perform daily under the big top.

Undercover thrills In 1993 the Adventuredome was added, said to be the biggest indoor theme

Try Adventuredome's thrilling rides, if you dare; Lucky the clown greets people at the big top (bottom left); bumper to bumper in the Adventuredome (bottom right)

park in the country, covering about 5 acres (2ha) beneath an enormous glass dome. The main thrill rides (for the very brave) include the Canyon Blaster, a massive double-loop, double-corkscrew roller coaster that achieves a top speed of 55mph (88kph); Chaos, which hurls its passengers in all directions as it speeds on its unpredictable course; and the Inverter, which literally turns your world upside down. If you enjoy getting very wet, head for the Rim Runner, a water ride that includes a breathtaking plunge. Equally thrilling is the IMAX Ridefilm Cineplex.

Gentler fun There are less stressful rides and activities, too, to please all ages. These include team laser tag and a climbing wall, while younger children will love the carousels, bumper cars and miniature golf.

THE BASICS

www.circuscircus.com

➕ E6

✉ 2880 Las Vegas Boulevard South

☎ 702/734-0410. Adventuredome: 702/794-3939

🕐 Midway Circus Acts: every half-hour 11am–midnight. Adventuredome: Mon–Thu 10–6, Fri, Sat 10am–midnight, Sun 10–9 (hours may vary seasonally)

🍴 Several cafés and restaurants

🚌 Deuce; Strip trolley

♿ Adventuredome: free admission, charge for rides; daily pass expensive

NASCAR Café and Speed: The Ride

Speed (left) at the NASCAR Café bursts out into Sahara Avenue (right)

THE BASICS

www.nascarcafelasvegas.com

➕ F6

✉ Sahara, 2535 Las Vegas Boulevard South

☎ 702/734-7223

🕐 Cyber Speedway: Sun–Thu 10–midnight, Fri, at 10–10. Speed: Sun–Thu 10–midnight, Fri, Sat 11am–1

🚌 Sahara

🚏 Deuce; Strip trolley

♿ Day pass: moderate

❓ You must be at least 54in (1.37m) tall to ride the Cyber Speedway

HIGHLIGHTS

● Meet the racing drivers when they are in town
● Cyber Speedway
● SPEED: The Ride

People are racing to this motor-sport theme café, with its state-of-the-art simulators, real stock cars, 3-D racing movies and the fastest roller coaster in the world winding in and out of the building.

NASCAR Café To call it a café hardly gives an accurate impression of this massive venue and its exciting attractions. But café it is, with 400 seats and an all-American menu. In addition, though, there are some amazing motor-racing exhibits, focusing on "Carzilla," the world's largest stock car. The upper level has eight regular-size stock cars suspended from the ceiling in racing formation, and there are about a dozen more cars around the place. While you munch on your lunch you can watch staff carry out a 20-second pitstop and see NASCAR news and driver profiles on giant screens. Would-be racing drivers can then try out their skills on the Las Vegas Cyber Speedway, where model stock cars are mounted on hydraulic bases with plenty of controls to personalize the ride.

Speed: The Ride Inside the café you can climb aboard this roller coaster, the fastest in the world, going from 0 to 40mph (64kph) in about two seconds, then accelerating to 70mph (113kph) as it bursts out of the building onto Sahara Avenue. The ride features a plunge through a tunnel, an exhilarating loop, a quick trip through the Sahara marquee and a stop at 224ft (68m) above ground…and then you cover the whole track again in reverse. This is not for the fainthearted, and is perhaps best experienced before you eat lunch!

Beam us up Scotty (right), the USS Enterprise is ready to depart from the Hilton

Star Trek:
The Experience

Enter (as boldly as you like) into the spirit of this out-of-this-world attraction and you'll have enormous fun. Dedicated Trekkies will, of course, find themselves in absolute heaven.

Beam me up Yes, you really are beamed aboard a re-creation of the USS *Enterprise*, to be greeted on the bridge by various crew members. Here you are issued your mission, then escorted into the TurboLift and along the Grand Corridor to the Shuttle Bay to board a 27-seat spacecraft. It's all a big build-up for an exciting high-speed simulator journey through the distant galaxies. If you don't fancy this stomach-churning chase, there is the Borg Invasion 4-D—a 3-D film with state-of-the-art audiovisual effects.

History of the Future Museum Back on terra firma, you can have a look around this huge collection of the actual props and memorabilia used in the nine *Star Trek* movies and four TV series. There are crew uniforms, some of the costumes and makeup that created the various weird and wonderful alien beings, special effects, stage props and weaponry, totaling more than 200 items.

Deep Space Nine Promenade This is a slightly different retail space with a range of *Star Trek* theme stuff to buy, from props and collectibles to crafted jewelry and art. You can outfit the family in *Star Trek* uniforms or buy celebrity cardboard cutouts. When you need refreshment, the Quark's Bar & Restaurant is on hand.

THE BASICS

www.startrekexp.com

🔲 F7

✉ Las Vegas Hilton, 3000 Paradise Road

☎ 702/697-8750

🕐 Daily 11.30–9.30 (hours vary seasonally)

🍽 Restaurant and bar

🚍 Las Vegas Hilton

🚌 108

💳 Combo ticket: expensive

❓ You must be at least 42in (1.06m) tall to go on the motion-simulator ride

---

HIGHLIGHTS

● Borg Invasion 4-D
● Klingon Encounter
● Museum exhibits

Stratosphere Tower

It might have been a tall order building the Stratosphere Tower, but wow, what a view

THE BASICS

www.stratospherehotel.com

➕ F5

✉ 2000 Las Vegas Boulevard South

☎ 702/380-7777

🎡 Rides: Sun–Thu 10am–1am, Fri, Sat 10am–2am (hours vary seasonally)

🍽 Top of the World restaurant; snack bar

🚌 Deuce; Strip trolley

♿ Tower: moderate (no charge if you have a restaurant reservation). Individual rides, including admission to tower: moderate. Multiride ticket: expensive

❓ You must be at least 48in (1.22m) tall to ride the Big Shot, and 54in (1.38m) to ride X-Scream and Insanity

HIGHLIGHTS

● The view from the observation deck

● A gourmet meal in the Top of the World restaurant

● The thrill rides

If zooming up the tallest free-standing tower in the United States isn't exciting enough for you, the highest thrill rides in the world await you at the top, along with a revolving restaurant and breathtaking views.

On top of the world Marking the northern end of the Strip, the Stratosphere stands in the shadow of its 1,149ft (350m) tower, which is the main attraction. By means of speedy double-decker elevators, you can be at the 12-floor complex known as the pod, which sits at the 775ft (236m) level, in less than 30 seconds and enjoy the spectacular view, either from the indoor, climate-controlled observation lounge or the open-air deck. Beneath this is the revolving Top of the World gourmet restaurant (▷ 82).

High-level thrills, low-level fun The quest for the ultimate in excitement led the owners of the Stratosphere to install attractions at the top of the tower that are definitely not for anyone who suffers from vertigo. Big Shot, 921ft (281m) high, propels passengers upward at 45mph (72kph), creating a G-force of four, then plummets at zero gravity. X-Scream dangles you off the side of the building, 100 levels up, while Insanity is the ultimate in thrill rides—you experience centrifugal forces of three Gs while being spun out 64ft (19m) beyond the edge of the tower 900ft (274m) up. At the foot of the tower is a 1960s-style funfair with a carousel, a Ferris wheel and a toned-down version of Big Shot for kids—called Little Shot.

Whenever Cupid strikes, a Las Vegas chapel is a memorable place to tie the knot

Whether your ideal wedding is being married by Elvis, tying the knot in a hot-air balloon, going for the quick drive-through ceremony or just a traditional approach, Vegas will have a chapel that can oblige.

What your heart desires Many hotels have elegant wedding chapels, or you can opt for an outdoor location amid majestic Nevada mountains and canyons. Anything goes in Las Vegas. If you're going to the chapel and you're going to get married, then some of the chapels north of Sahara Avenue will provide a day to remember.

Gathered together in the sight of Elvis The Graceland Chapel and the Viva Las Vegas Wedding Chapel offer the most renowned style of wedding in Las Vegas, the ceremony that's conducted by an Elvis look-alike.

Chapel of the Bells Follow in the footsteps of Mickey Rooney, football legend Pelé and soldiers marrying before Desert Storm in this most polished of venues. Among their promotions are a free bottle of champagne and personalized wedding certificate.

Little White Chapel The setting of many celebrity weddings (including one of Joan Collins' marriages), with traditional ceremonies around the clock—simply show up and wait your turn. The Little White Chapel in the Sky marries couples in a hot-air balloon.

THE BASICS

Graceland Chapel
✚ G4 ✉ 619 Las Vegas Boulevard South
☎ 702/382-0091; www.gracelandchapel.com

Viva Las Vegas Wedding Chapel
✚ F4 ✉ 1205 Las Vegas Boulevard South
☎ 702/384-0771; www.vivalasvegas.com

Chapel of the Bells
✚ F5 ✉ 2233 Las Vegas Boulevard South
☎ 702/735-6803; www.chapelofthebells.lasvegas.com

Little White Chapel
✚ F4 ✉ 1301 Las Vegas Boulevard South
☎ 702/382-5943; www.littlewhitechapel.com

HIGHLIGHTS

● Each chapel has a wedding planner for a stress-free ceremony.
● Whatever the happy couple visualize can become reality.
● Couples can get married any time of day.

NORTH STRIP

★

TOP 25

More to See

AN EVENING AT THE CAGE

www.rivierahotel.com

This show elevated drag to an art form. The glittering cosmopolitan entertainment sees a cast of male impersonators transformed into unbelievably accurate representations of female superstars that might include Madonna, Cher or Diana Ross.

⊞ E7 ⊠ Riviera, 2901 Las Vegas Boulevard South ☎ 702/794-9433 ⏰ Wed–Mon 7.30pm 🚌 Deuce; Strip trolley 💷 Very expensive

WYNN LAS VEGAS

The doors eventually opened on this $2.7 billion, eagerly awaited hotel-casino in April 2005. The incredible resort, with its gleaming bronze tower, covers 215 acres (87ha) and is one of the tallest buildings in Las Vegas, towering 60 stories over the Strip. A lagoon backed by a 150ft (46m) man-made mountain, complete with waterfall, takes center stage. At intervals throughout the day a visual spectacular is projected on the water and on a screen that rises out of the lagoon. An evergreen oasis on the Strip, the gardens have the constant aroma of fresh flowers. The resort is set in its own 18-hole golf course (open to guests only), and features the Wynn Esplanade (▷ 80), which offers a distinctive collection of designer shops, complete with a full-size Ferrari-Maserati dealership where some of the hottest cars in the world are on show. Treat yourself to innovative spa treatments, fine dining and top-class entertainment like the aquatic spectacular, Le Rêve, which is the first show of its kind in Vegas. The Wynn Collection of Fine Art is Steve Wynn's personal collection of artwork. Central to the collection is Pablo Picasso's *Le Rêve*, but more gems on view include works by Matisse, Rembrandt, Monet, Renoir, Gauguin, Van Gogh and Warhol—a collection to rival many.

⊞ E7 ⊠ 3131 Las Vegas Boulevard South ☎ 702/770-7000 ⏰ Art collection: Tue–Sat 10–5, Sun 1–5 🚉 Las Vegas Convention Center 🚌 Deuce; Strip trolley 💷 Art collection: inexpensive

Le Rêve, at Wynn Las Vegas

The impressive Wynn Las Vegas

Shopping

BEBE

Sassy boutique selling sleek designs and curve-hugging wear inspired by the latest trends.

✚ D7 ⊠ Fashion Show Mall, 3200 Las Vegas Boulevard South ☎ 702/892-8083 🚍 Deuce; Strip trolley

BETSEY JOHNSON

Flowing fabrics with beaded and embroidered detail are the style at this wacky shop for a wacky clientele.

✚ D7 ⊠ Fashion Show Mall, 3200 Las Vegas Boulevard South ☎ 702/735-3338 🚍 Deuce; Strip trolley

BONANZA GIFTS

www.worldslargestgiftshop.co The self-styled "largest souvenir store in the world" has a mind-boggling array of tacky mementos, T-shirts and postcards. It's worth a visit, just to see how tasteless it can all get.

✚ E6 ⊠ 2440 Las Vegas Boulevard South ☎ 702/385-7359 🚍 Deuce; Strip trolley

COWTOWN BOOTS

www.cowtownboots.com Great Western clothing and cowboy boots, mostly at a good discount. The largest outlet of its kind in Nevada.

✚ F6 ⊠ 2989 South Paradise Road ☎ 702/737-8469 🚍 108

FASHION SHOW MALL

www.thefashionshow.com This mall has had a $362 million expansion and is among the largest in the US. Stores include Saks Fifth Avenue, Nordstrom, Macy's, Neiman Marcus and Bloomingdale's, and there are lots of eateries.

✚ D7 ⊠ 3200 Las Vegas Boulevard South ☎ 702/369-0704 🚍 Deuce; Strip trolley

MANOLO BLAHNIK

Timeless and beautifully made, Manolo's sexy shoes are as famous as the women who wear them.

✚ E7 ⊠ Wynn Las Vegas, 3131 Las Vegas Boulevard South ☎ 702/770-7000 🚍 Deuce; Strip trolley

OSCAR DE LA RENTA

This renowned designer, famous for his delicate and opulent collection of women's clothes and accessories, has chosen the Wynn Esplanade to display his finery.

✚ E7 ⊠ Wynn Las Vegas, 3131 Las Vegas Boulevard South ☎ 702/770-7000 🚍 Deuce; Strip trolley

JUST FOR FUN

There's no doubt about it, Las Vegas is chock-full of enough tacky souvenirs to be able to supply the rest of the world's major tourist spots. But this is Vegas after all, and kitsch is just another facet of its fun character. You can bet that not many people will leave without at least one item packed in their suitcase that announces to the world they have visited Sin City.

RED ROOSTER ANTIQUES MALL

Housed in a former bottling plant, this labyrinth of rooms conceals stands cluttered with postcards, casino memorabilia, 1950s furniture and more.

✚ E5 ⊠ 1109 Western Avenue ☎ 702/382-0067 🚍 Deuce; Strip trolley

SAM ASH

www.samashmusic.com This megastore is a musicians' playground, stacked high with guitars, amps, drums, and brass and wind instruments of every conceivable brand.

✚ H6 ⊠ 2747 Maryland Parkway ☎ 702/734-0007 🚍 109

SERGE'S SHOWGIRL WIGS

www.showgirlwigs.com This store has around 10,000 wigs, of all shapes, sizes and shades, and you can even top one with a showgirl headdress.

✚ G6 ⊠ Commercial Center Plaza, 953 East Sahara Avenue ☎ 702/732-1015 🚍 204

WYNN ESPLANADE

The endless list of exclusive names can't fail to impress at this new luxury hotel mall. The first Jean Paul Gaultier store in the US opened here and there is even a Ferrari and Maserati showroom.

✚ E7 ⊠ Wynn Las Vegas, 3131 Las Vegas Boulevard South ☎ 702/770-7000 🚇 Las Vegas Convention Center 🚍 Deuce; Strip trolley

Entertainment and Nightlife

THE BEACH
This loud, tropical-theme hot spot over two levels is built around a huge dance floor that is always crammed with fun-seekers. Bikini-clad girls and guys in surf shorts serve free shots of tequila.

➕ F1 ✉ 365 Convention Center Drive ☎ 702/731-1925 Ⓜ Las Vegas Hilton 🚌 108, Deuce; Strip trolley

CASBAR THEATER LOUNGE
www.saharavegas.com
This is a real throwback to the Las Vegas of the 1970s, before any of today's sophistication set in. There's live entertainment nightly.

➕ F6 ✉ Sahara, 2535 Las Vegas Boulevard South ☎ 702/737-2111 Ⓜ Sahara 🚌 Deuce; Strip trolley

COMEDY CLUB
www.rivierahotel.com
Four acts a night do stand-up at this comedy spot on the second floor of the Mardi Gras Plaza at the Riviera. Once a month the venue holds a late-night show for X-rated comedians.

➕ E6 ✉ Riviera, 2901 Las Vegas Boulevard South ☎ 702/794-9433 🚌 Deuce; Strip trolley

CONGO SHOWROOM
www.saharavegas.com
A lively schedule of musicians and comedians is on the bill here.

➕ F6 ✉ Sahara, 2535 Las Vegas Boulevard South

☎ 702/737-2111 Ⓜ Sahara 🚌 Deuce; Strip trolley

FLYAWAY INDOOR SKYDIVING
www.flyawayindoorskydiving.com
Test your skills at this exciting new sporting challenge. A vertical wind tunnel simulates the freefall experience of skydiving in a column of air with vertical airspeeds up to 120mph (193kph). No experience is needed; you can book a single flight session or a personalized coaching program.

➕ F7 ✉ 200 Convention Center Drive ☎ 702/731-4768 Ⓜ Las Vegas Hilton 🚌 108, Deuce; Strip trolley

LAS VEGAS HILTON SHOWROOM
www.lvhilton.com
A variety of musicians, comedians and magicians perform here and tickets are reasonably priced.

➕ F7 ✉ Las Vegas Hilton, 3000 Paradise Road ☎ 702/732-5755 Ⓜ Las Vegas Hilton 🚌 108

HEADLINERS
Headliners come and go in the city, some staying longer than others. But Las Vegas likes to keep its future big names under wraps, so you never know what's lined up. Recent superstars who have performed here include U2, Paul McCartney and Barry Manilow. As shows can close just like that, it is always best to check before turning up.

LURE
www.wynnlasvegas.com
A seductive atmosphere and glamorous surroundings, where cocktails, champagne and spirits flow freely, is what draws an A-list crowd to this ultralounge at the Wynn before heading off to Tryst nightclub (▷ below). Dress to impress if you want to be noticed.

➕ E7 ✉ Wynn Las Vegas, 3131 Las Vegas Boulevard South ☎ 702/770-3633 🚌 Deuce; Strip trolley

PEPPERMILL'S FIRE-SIDE LOUNGE
www.peppermilllasvegas.com
Shag carpeting, fire pits, enormous white silk flowers and indoor fountains are still the rage at this tribute to old-world Vegas.

➕ E7 ✉ 2985 Las Vegas Boulevard South ☎ 702/735-4177 🚌 Deuce; Strip trolley

TRYST
www.wynnlasvegas.com
Rapidly becoming one of the most enticing nightclubs in the city, tantalizing Tryst sets a new trend for nightlife in Las Vegas. Sophisticated deep-red and black combinations enhance intimate booth-style seating and the open-air, sizable dance floor extends into a 90-ft (27m) waterfall that cascades into a lagoon.

➕ E7 ✉ Wynn Las Vegas, 3131 Las Vegas Boulevard South ☎ 702/770-3375 🚌 Deuce; Strip trolley

NORTH STRIP

ENTERTAINMENT AND NIGHTLIFE

Restaurants

NORTH STRIP

Prices are approximate, based on a 3-course meal for one person.
$$$ over $50
$$ $20–$50
$ under $20

ANDIAMO ($$$)

www.lvhilton.com
Brightly lit, with lots of fresh flowers, this is a popular, fairly casual restaurant serving fine northern Italian cuisine.
✚ F7 ✉ Las Vegas Hilton, 3000 Paradise Road
☎ 702/732-5755 ⏰ Daily 5.30–11 🚾 Las Vegas Hilton
🚌 108

BRASSERIE BOULUD ($$$)

www.wynnlasvegas.com
Chef Daniel Boulud brings his mastery of French cuisine to this bustling brasserie overlooking the lagoon. Large windows separate the room into intimate sections. You will need a reservation for a seat on the coveted patio.
✚ E7 ✉ Wynn Las Vegas, 3131 Las Vegas Boulevard South ☎ 702/248-DINE
⏰ Daily 5.30–10 🚾 Deuce; Strip trolley

ENVY ($$$)

www.envysteakhouse.com
Richard Chamberlain, one of America's leading chefs, uses top-quality, fresh ingredients in his innovative dishes, which redefine the traditional steak-house offerings. Dark wood and soothing red shades give a warm, sophisticated feel.
✚ F7 ✉ Renaissance, 3400 Paradise Road ☎ 702/784-5816 ⏰ Daily 7–3, 5–10.30
🚾 Las Vegas Hilton 🚌 108

KRISTOFER'S ($$)

www.rivierahotel.com
The great steaks, tender ribs and broiled chicken in butter served here is matched by great prices; the barbecue sauce is wonderful, too.
✚ E6 ✉ Riviera, 2901 Las Vegas Boulevard South ☎ 702/794-9376 ⏰ Daily 5–10 🚾 Deuce; Strip trolley

LOTUS OF SIAM ($)

www.saipinchutima.com
The Lotus is one of only a few Thai restaurants in Las Vegas, and has a huge menu of tasty dishes. Let them know how hot you like your food and they'll prepare it accordingly. If you overdo it, have the coconut ice cream for dessert.

DINING WITH A VIEW

There are some wonderful spots in Vegas where you can savor great views while you eat, but one of the best is the Top of the World restaurant (▷ this page). Located on the 106th floor of the Stratosphere Tower, it makes one revolution in 60 minutes, during which you can see the Strip, the mountains, the valleys and beyond.

✚ G6 ✉ 953 East Sahara Avenue ☎ 702/735-3033
⏰ Mon–Fri 11.30–2.30, 5.30–9.30, Sat, Sun 5.30–10 🚌 204

RA ($$)

www.rasushi.com
An upbeat, casual mood creates the perfect setting to enjoy fresh sushi, Japanese-fusion cuisine and signature dishes so good that you can't wait to return. Bright wall hangings and globe lighting accent the interior.
✚ D7 ✉ Fashion Show Mall, 3200 Las Vegas Boulevard South ☎ 702/696-0008
⏰ Daily 11–midnight

THE STEAKHOUSE ($$)

www.circuscircus.com
This old-timer is popular for its succulent prime ribs and tasty grilled steaks, all at low prices. There's seafood, lobster, chicken and lamb as well.
✚ E6 ✉ Circus Circus, 2880 Las Vegas Boulevard South ☎ 702/794-3767 ⏰ Sun–Fri 5–10, Sat 5–11 🚌 Deuce; Strip trolley

TOP OF THE WORLD ($$$)

www.topoftheworld.com
Enjoy delicious culinary creations in this revolving restaurant 833ft (254m) above the Strip. However, the great view comes at sky-high prices.
✚ F5 ✉ Stratosphere Tower, 2000 Las Vegas Boulevard South ☎ 702/380-7711
⏰ Sun–Thu 11–3, 5.30–10.30, Fri, Sat 11–3, 5.30–11
🚌 Deuce; Strip trolley

Evolving from the early saloons, the first casino-hotels were built downtown in the early 1930s. Now, in the shade of the booming Strip, projects such as the Fremont Street Experience have helped it keep pace.

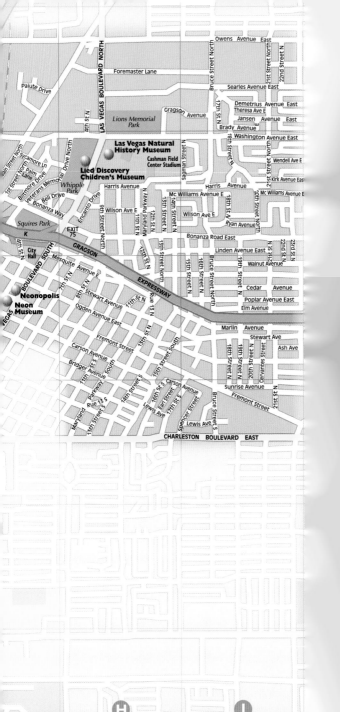

Downtown

HIGHLIGHTS

● Fremont Street Experience
(▷ 88)
● Main Street Station
● Golden Nugget Casino
(▷ 90)
● The Arts Factory

TIPS

● Some of the carts around
Fremont have unusual gift
items for sale.
● Go to the Golden Gate at
Fremont and Main streets to
sample the hotel's famous
99-cent shrimp cocktail.

**With its old-world appeal, Downtown is
where the spirit of Las Vegas' humble
beginnings still lives on through original
casino hotels like the Plaza, Golden
Nugget and Golden Gate.**

Origins Centered on Fremont Street between Main
and 9th, the streets of Downtown are narrower,
more low-key and less glamorous than the Strip.
In the 1920s, Fremont Street was the first street in
Las Vegas to be paved and have traffic lights, and
by the 1930s it had the first licensed gaming hall.
Downtown already had 36 years of history as the
commercial heart of Vegas by the time the first casino resort, El Rancho, was built on the Strip in 1941.

Revitalization Downtown had lost much of its
business to the Strip by the 1990s, when Vegas

Mermaids Casino (top left); historic downtown hotels such as the Golden Gate (top right, below right) and the Plaza (below middle left) are an interesting reminder of the city's frontier history; antique slot machine (below middle right) and detail of a glass window (below left), both displayed at the Golden Gate

entrepreneur Steve Wynn and fellow hoteliers set about reinventing the area. They came up with the $70 million Fremont Street Experience (▷ 88), which succeeded in bringing in the punters once again and putting Glitter Gulch—as it is known— firmly back on the map.

More attractions With its striking Victorian decor and genuine antiques, Main Street Station (▷ 109) has one of the city's best casinos in terms of comfort and atmosphere, and it's smoke-free. The Arts Factory is a collection of artists, architects, photographers and graphic designers exhibiting in galleries under one roof in the Gateway Arts District. You can experience more creative talent at First Friday, with live performances and other activities on the first Friday of each month. A welcome addition in 2004 was the Neonopolis mall (▷ 90).

THE BASICS

☐ G3
✉ Centered around Fremont and Main streets
🍴 Numerous
🚌 108, Deuce

Fremont Street Experience

Fremont Street ablaze after dark (left); Fremont hotel, a downtown institution (right)

THE BASICS

www.vegasexperience.com

⊞ G3

✉ Fremont Street

☎ 702/678-5600

🕐 Every hour on the hour 6pm–midnight

🚌 108, Deuce

♿ Free

DID YOU KNOW?

● Fremont Street was the hub of Las Vegas for nearly four decades.

● Each column supporting the overhead structure carries 400,000lb (181,440kg) of weight.

● The components for the light show produce 65,536 color combinations.

● The show's sound system generates 540,000 watts.

Head north to the Downtown area after dark to see the only show of its kind in the world—a fantastic sound-and-light show on a massive frame that overarches a five-block area.

High-tech marvel The specifications for the components of this display are impressive—2 million light bulbs, 180 strobe lights, 64 variable-hued lighting installations producing a whole spectrum of shades, over 30 moving, tilting mirrors that further increase the effect by reflecting the lights, and a state-of-the-art sound system that broadcasts concert-quality music through more than 200 speakers. The whole show is controlled by 126 computers, each with a capacity equal to 100 home PCs.

Under cover of lightness This glittering spectacular is based on a huge, solid frame that curves 90ft (27m) above traffic-free Fremont Street, between Main and 4th streets, covering an area of more than 4 acres (1.5ha). A number of the Downtown casinos are within this area, adding to the overall effect with their illuminated facades. There are 16 massive columns and 43,000 struts supporting the frame, but once the show starts you are totally focused on this breathtaking experience that has been wowing the crowds here since 1995.

By day You might suppose that, by comparison, it's rather dull here during the day. But the display frame shelters a lively shopping mall, the sound system continues to pipe in music to shop by, and there are often free concerts and street performers.

Porcupines, lions and zebras are just some of the creatures that feature here

Las Vegas Natural History Museum

This terrific museum provides a welcome contrast to the high life and glitz of the shows and casinos. There are lots of interactive displays, live animals to pet, animatronic dinosaurs and much more.

Unique items When you consider all the museums in the United States, you might not expect a Las Vegas institution to have something the others don't. However, among the displays here are two particularly rare species—the African water chevrotain (a cross between a pig and a deer) and the Liberian zebra duiker. In addition, there are more than 26 species of stuffed animals mounted in cases, including the largest jaguar ever displayed.

Marine world Opened in 2004, the whales exhibit is part of the Marine Life Gallery and complements the shark displays featuring live leopard sharks and a shark egg hatchery. There is a scale model of an orca, also known as the killer whale, a melonhead whale and a beluga whale, complete with baby. You can learn about the behavior and conservation of these creatures. Don't miss the re-creation of the jaws of a 50ft-long (15m) prehistoric shark.

Fun with the animals Many of the displays are animated, including five robotic dinosaurs—the 35ft (10.5m) T-rex is very popular. There are also live animals that visitors are occasionally allowed to pet. The concept is to combine education with fun, and the interactive area is a great place for children to try out their skills as amateur archaeologists and paleontologists.

THE BASICS

www.lvnhm.org

✚ H2

✉ 900 North Las Vegas Boulevard

☎ 702/384-3466

🕙 Daily 9–4

🚌 113

♿ Inexpensive

HIGHLIGHTS

● Hands-on activity room
● Whales exhibition
● Marine Life Gallery
● Robotic T-rex and Dinosaur Gallery
● African Galleries

DOWNTOWN ★ **TOP 25**

TOP 25

More to See

GOLDEN NUGGET
www.goldennugget.com
For a touch of nostalgia, come to one of the city's originals, opened in 1946. What this casino lacks in Vegas panache it more than makes up for in class.
➕ G3 ⊠ 129 East Fremont Street ☎ 702/385-7111 🕐 Daily 24 hours 🚌 108, Deuce

LIED DISCOVERY CHILDREN'S MUSEUM
www.ldcm.org
This hands-on approach to learning is not just for children, as there is plenty to stimulate adults, too. Constantly changing exhibits introduce children to different careers, from banking to mining. There are also exhibits of Las Vegas' most famous neon signs.
➕ H2 ⊠ 833 Las Vegas Boulevard North ☎ 702/382-3445 🕐 Tue–Fri 9–4, Sat 10–5, Sun 12–5 🚌 113 🖐 Inexpensive

NEON MUSEUM
www.neonmuseum.org
The museum's mission is "to collect, preserve, study and exhibit neon signs." This is, in fact, an outdoor self-guided walking tour on and around Fremont Street. Some of the city's famed neon signs dating back to 1940 are displayed as installation artworks on, or just off, Fremont Street. Call for details.
➕ G3 ⊠ Fremont Street ☎ 702/387-6366 🚌 108, Deuce 🖐 Free

NEONOPOLIS
www.neonopolis.net
Apart from the usual shops, eating and drinking options, this entertainment metropolis has an art gallery, a 14-screen movie theater, and live entertainment on the center stage Friday and Saturday evenings. Play air hockey and sample the latest ride simulators or play a few games of pool after you've tested your skills at bowling.
➕ G3 ⊠ 450 Fremont Street ☎ 702/477-0470 🕐 Sun–Thu 11–9, Fri, Sat 11–10

VEGAS VIC AND VEGAS VICKI
These nostalgic neon signs are part of the Downtown's history; Vic is perched on top of the Pioneer Club and Vicki on the Girls of Glitter Gulch.
➕ G3 ⊠ Fremont Street 🚌 108, Deuce

The elegant Golden Nugget inside (right) and out (above)

Around Fremont Street

Begin just as dusk falls, walking through a historic part of the city past some of the early buildings, and finishing in a blaze of neons.

DISTANCE: 1 mile (1.5km) **ALLOW:** 2 hours

START

EL CORTEZ HOTEL
➕ G3 🚌 108, Deuce

END

WEE KIRK O'HEATHER
➕ G3 🚌 108, Deuce

① Start at the El Cortez, the only downtown property whose exterior has remained mostly unaltered. Turn right onto Las Vegas Boulevard. Proceed to Stewart Avenue and turn left.

⑧ Go right and walk a few hundred yards to the Wee Kirk O'Heather Wedding Chapel on the left, now one of the oldest operating chapels.

② About halfway up on the right is the Post Office/Federal Building–a neoclassical structure built in 1933. Continue to the top and at the T-junction with Main Street you will see Main Street Station hotel (▷ 109).

⑦ Look out for the neon signs Vegas Vic and Vegas Vickie (▷ 90). Stay for the sound-and-light show before proceeding to the end. On the left is Neonopolis (▷ 90). At the intersection with Las Vegas Boulevard are old refurbished signs such as Aladdin's Lamp and the Hacienda Horse and Rider.

③ Inside is a collection of antiques—pick up a map at the front desk and take a self-guided tour. Continue along Main Street. On the right is an antique rail car that served as a personal car for Buffalo Bill Cody and Annie Oakley.

⑥ Turn down Fremont Street (▷ 88) under the huge canopy. As you walk down, on the right is the Golden Nugget (▷ 90), left is Binion's Horseshoe and next left is the Fremont, three of downtown's most nostalgic hotel casinos.

④ Next on the right you come to the Union Plaza hotel, where the Union Pacific Railroad Depot stood, once the focal point of downtown.

⑤ Cross the road to the Golden Gate, one of the oldest remaining hotels in the area.

DOWNTOWN · **WALK**

Shopping

THE ATTIC
www.atticvintage.com
Feel like you're a child again rummaging through grandma's attic at this fascinating place. There is a hidden treasure in every corner, including a good range of retro and vintage clothing, interesting collectibles, furniture, jewelry, old radios, TVs, cameras and electrical appliances.
✚ F3 ✉ 1018 South Main Street ☎ 702/388-4088
🚌 108

FUNK HOUSE
www.funkhouselasvegas.com
One of the best antiques stores in the city is the creation of Cindy Funkhouser. Her growing collection includes some interesting items from the late-1950s and early-1960s including furniture, glass, jewelry, rugs, paintings and toys.
✚ F4 ✉ 1228 South Casino Center Boulevard
☎ 702/678-6278 🚌 108

GAMBLER'S BOOK SHOP
www.gamblersbook.com
This specialist bookstore has all the references you might need to prepare you for a flutter, whether it be at the tables or at the track. Don't be tempted by the video tutorials on cheating—casino staff are all too familiar with them. There is game software also on sale in this shop.
✚ H3 ✉ 630 South 11th Street ☎ 702/382-7555
🚌 109, 206

GAMBLER'S GENERAL STORE
What better souvenir of a trip to Las Vegas than something with a gambling theme? Impress your friends with a roulette wheel, blackjack table or slot machine. The used-card decks and gambling chips from major casinos are good, inexpensive buys.
✚ F3 ✉ 800 South Main Street ☎ 702/382-9903
🚌 108

LAS VEGAS PAPER DOLLS
www.lvpaperdoll.com
Lovely stationery shop with items by top designers. Look for the roses of artist F. B. Fogg, who uses an ancient Egyptian

ANTIQUES TRAIL
Believe it or not, Las Vegas has accumulated quite a few antiques stores over the years, most of them in the Downtown area around the east end of Charleston Boulevard. Here, knowledgeable antiques dealers have set up shop in tiny 1930s converted houses lining both sides of the street. If you stop off first at Silver Horse Antiques (▷ this page), you can collect a map that shows you where all the other shops are located and lists their opening times.

paper-making technique in her colorful work.
✚ F4 ✉ 231 West Charleston Boulevard
☎ 702/385-7892 🚌 206

LAS VEGAS PREMIUM OUTLETS
www.premiumoutlets.com
There can't be many names missing from the 120 designer and name-brand outlet stores housed here: Ann Taylor, Dolce and Gabbana, Guess, Adidas, Elie Tahari, the list goes on. Shop until you drop and save 25 to 65 percent in the process.
✚ F3 ✉ 875 South Grand Central Parkway ☎ 702/474-7500 🚌 106, 108 from DTC

SILVER HORSE ANTIQUES
Take a look at this fascinating store with lamps, furniture, glass and collectibles among a few of the items hidden in this treasure house.
✚ H4 ✉ 1651 East Charleston Boulevard
☎ 702/385-2700 🚌 206

TOYS OF YESTER-YEAR
This tiny little place will take you back a few years with its wonderful collection of lovely old train sets, wind-up toys, dolls and books.
✚ H4 ✉ 2028 East Charleston Boulevard
☎ 702/598-4030 🚌 206

Restaurants

PRICES

Prices are approximate, based on a 3-course meal for one person.
$$$ over $50
$$ $20–$50
$ under $20

BINION'S COFFEE SHOP ($)

www.binions.com
This is a great place for a light snack or something more substantial at a low price. The generous breakfasts are particularly good.
➕ G3 ✉ Binion's Horseshoe, 128 Fremont Street ☎ 702/382-1600 🕐 Daily 24 hours 🚌 108, Deuce

BINION'S RANCH STEAKHOUSE ($$$)

www.binions.com
Settle down to the delicious succulent steaks and chops that are served amid the attractive Victorian decor, while taking in the spectacular views.
➕ G3 ✉ Binion's Horseshoe, 128 East Fremont Street ☎ 702/382-1600 🕐 Daily 5–11 🚌 108, Deuce

DONA MARIA TAMALES ($)

Certainly best here are the great *tamales*— shredded chicken, beef and pork wrapped in cornmeal.
➕ G4 ✉ 910 Las Vegas Boulevard South ☎ 702/382-6538 🕐 Mon–Fri 8–10 🚌 Deuce

GARDEN COURT ($)

www.mainstreetcasino.com
Watch your food being prepared at what is said to be Downtown's best buffet. On the nine counters are American, Pacific Rim, Chinese and Mexican dishes.
➕ G2 ✉ Main Street Station, 200 North Main Street ☎ 702/ 387-1896 🕐 Daily 7–10.30, 11–3, 4–10 🚌 108, Deuce

HUGO'S CELLAR ($$$)

www.hugoscellar.com
Below street level, this romantic restaurant has a touch of class. Each female receives a red rose as she enters the dimly lit, dark-wood space. Excellent Continental cuisine; some dishes are prepared at the table. Expect lots of pampering.
➕ G3 ✉ Queens Hotel, 202 Fremont Street ☎ 702/385-4011 🕐 Daily 5–10.30 🚌 108, Deuce

DIAMOND RATINGS

Restaurants in the US are inspected and evaluated for quality of food, service, decor and ambience by the AAA's tourism editors. Ratings range from one diamond, for a simple, family-oriented eatery, to five diamonds, for restaurants with the highest standards of service and outstanding culinary skills.

LILLIE'S NOODLE HOUSE ($$)

www.goldennugget.com
There's an odd mix of cultures at work here, but the cuisine is most definitely Chinese, and the Sichuan and Cantonese dishes are of exceptional quality.
➕ G3 ✉ Golden Nugget, 129 East Fremont Street ☎ 702/385-7111 🕐 Tue–Thu 6pm–midnight, Fri, Sat 6pm–1am 🚌 108, Deuce

LIMERICKS ($$)

www.fitzgeraldslasvegas.com
Comfy booths in an atmosphere reminiscent of an English gentleman's club. There are fine prime ribs and steaks, fresh seafood and lamb, and desserts made at the in-house bakery.
➕ G3 ✉ Fitzgeralds, 301 Fremont Street ☎ 702/388-2400 🕐 Thu–Mon 5–11 🚌 108, Deuce

SECOND STREET GRILL ($$)

www.fremontcasino.com
Step back in time at this hidden gem and sample good Pacific rim and contemporary cuisine at affordable prices. Soft lighting and rich woods encourage you to relax in the oversized chairs.
➕ G3 ✉ 200 Fremont Street ☎ 702/385-3232 🕐 Sun, Mon, Thu 6–10, Fri, Sat 6–11 🚌 108, Deuce

DOWNTOWN

RESTAURANTS

Farther Afield

It's hard to imagine that such a short distance from Vegas is a world of natural beauty. Interesting geological formations, spectacular scenery and a varied wildlife are light years away from the razzmatazz.

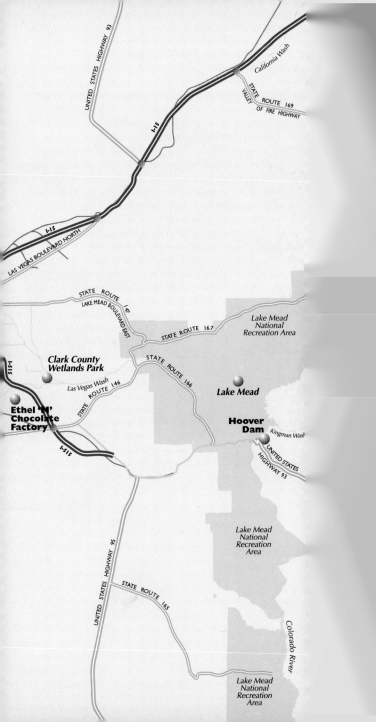

Hoover Dam and Lake Mead

TOP
25

It's hard to visit Vegas without feeling some wonderment about the power it must take to light up the town. You'll find some answers at Hoover Dam, and while you're out of the city, enjoy a cruise on the lovely lake it created.

A marvel of engineering Without the Hoover Dam, Las Vegas, as we know it, would not exist. Constructed in the mid-1930s to control flooding on the Colorado River, it also provides drinking water for 25 million people and electricity for half a million homes. It was a massive undertaking that was, amazingly, completed two years ahead of schedule. At the peak of construction, over 5,000 people were employed and 96 workers died on the project. Fascinating tours take visitors deep inside the structure to learn about its inner workings.

Hoover Dam's structural volume surpasses that of the largest pyramid in Egypt (left); Lake Mohave, encompassed in the Lake Mead National Recreation Area (bottom middle); men at work—the dam is considered one of the seven engineering wonders of the world (top middle); fireworks over Lake Mead (right)

Lovely Lake Mead The damming of the Colorado River between 1935 and 1938 created the second-largest artificial lake in the United States, with a 550-mile (885km) shoreline. There's a scenic drive along the western side, and the Alan Bible Visitor Center, just west of the dam, has lots of useful information about water-borne activities. There are five marinas, and you can rent a boat or jet ski, do some fishing, go water-skiing or swimming. On dry land there are pleasurable lakeshore walks and facilities for camping and picnicking. A great way to see the lake is from one of the many boat trips that are available, which include breakfast, lunch, dinner and dinner-dance cruises. Boulder City, on the lake shore, is an interesting place that was built to house dam construction workers and remains "dry" (no alcohol or gambling) to this day.

THE BASICS

www.usbr.gov/lc/hoover dam; www.nps.gov/lame
🔛 Off map at J1
✉ 30 miles (48km) southeast of Las Vegas
☎ Hoover Dam tours: 702/494-2517; Alan Bible Visitor Center: 702/293-8990; Lake Mead Cruises: 702/294-6180
🕐 Hoover Dam Visitor Center: daily 9–4; Alan Bible Visitor Center: daily 9–4.15
💷 Hoover Dam Visitor Center and tours: moderate. Lake Mead Recreation Area: inexpensive; Lake Mead cruise: moderate

Red Rock Canyon

HIGHLIGHTS

● Scenic Loop
● Hiking trails
● Children's Discovery Trail
● Wildlife–burros (wild donkeys) and mountain lions (hard to spot)

TIPS

● Don't feed the wildlife; the burros may bite or kick.
● Take plenty of water if hiking–the heat can be fierce–and wear extra layers in winter.

This canyon was created 65 million years ago when the Keystone Thrust Fault pushed one rock plate up over another. The resulting spectacular formations, in contrasting gray limestone and red sandstone, are awesome.

Focal point It's incredible to think that this striking canyon, set in the 197,000-acre (79,725ha) Red Rock Canyon National Conservation Area, is a mere 20-minute drive from the razzmatazz of Vegas. The focal point is the steep red rock escarpment more than 13 miles (21km) long and almost 3,000ft (915m) high. More canyons have been gouged out within the formation by constant snowmelt and rains, creating the present dramatic landscape. In contrast to the dry desert, springs and streams encourage lush vegetation.

Whatever way you choose to travel through Red Rock Canyon, on foot, by car or bicycle, there are breathtaking vistas all around

Planning ahead The best place to start is at the Red Rock Visitor Center, which offers information and interpretation about all the recreational opportunities available, including hiking and climbing. It also has a recorded self-guide tour giving you a description of the geology and wildlife (all protected) in the area, and provides maps of hiking and bicycle trails and details of picnic sites. Park rangers are also on hand to give advice. Climbing should be undertaken only by experts with the correct equipment. Stick to the trails and be aware of weather conditions—flash floods do occur.

Loop the loop For those staying in their cars, the 13-mile (21km) one-way Scenic Loop, leaving from the Visitor Center, gives the chance to see some of the best rock formations and to pause for photos at the Calico Vista viewpoints.

THE BASICS

www.nv.blm.gov/
redrockcanyon
➕ Off map at A4
✉ South Nevada,
20 miles (32km) west of
Las Vegas
☎ Red Rock Visitor
Center: 702/515-5350
🕐 Red Rock Visitor
Center: daily 8–4.30
👣 Parking: inexpensive;
free for hikers

More to See

CLARK COUNTY WETLANDS PARK

www.co.clark.nv.us/parks

Just 8 miles (13km) east of the Strip, this environmentally conscious park has a visitor center where you can pick up trail maps. Bird-watching is popular here, with recorded species including great blue herons, snowy egrets and black bellied whistling ducks.

➕ Off map at J10 ✉ 7050 Wetlands Park Lane ☎ 702/455-7522 🕔 Visitor center: daily 9–3. Nature center: daily dawn–dusk 🚌 202, then walk 1 mile (1.5km) 👪 Free

ETHEL M. CHOCOLATE FACTORY

www.ethelm.com

Take a self-guiding audio tour to discover how Ethel Mars' huge chocolate enterprise began and get an insight into the production processes. At the end sample your favorite candy.

➕ Off map at J11 ✉ 2 Cactus Garden Drive, Henderson (8 miles/5km southeast of Las Vegas) ☎ 702/435-2641 🕔 Daily 8.30–7 🚌 217 👪 Free

LAS VEGAS ART MUSEUM

www.lasvegasartmuseum.org

Housed in a first-rate exhibition space attached to the Sahara West Library, this museum is dedicated to bringing quality art exhibitions to the community. The LVAM moved to its present premises in 1997 and is now affiliated with the Smithsonian Museum.

➕ Off map at A6 ✉ 9600 West Sahara Avenue ☎ 702/360-8000 🕔 Tue–Sat 10–5, Sun 1–5 🚌 204 👪 Inexpensive

NEVADA STATE MUSEUM

In a tranquil setting in Lorenzi Park, about 5 miles (8km) from the Strip, is the State Museum and Historical Society, dedicated to advancement of the knowledge of history and natural history of Nevada. Learn about life before Vegas, and view exhibits of dinosaurs and early man right through to the controversial nuclear testing program. Photographic displays of Las Vegas in the early years are on show.

➕ B2 ✉ 700 Twin Lakes Drive ☎ 702/486-5205 🕔 Daily 9–5 🚌 106, 208 👪 Inexpensive

Cactus garden at Ethel M's

Get back to nature at Clark County Wetlands Park

Excursions

THE BASICS

www.nps.gov/grca
Distance: South Rim 260 miles (418km) from Las Vegas; North Rim 275 miles (443km)
✉ South Rim Visitor Center: opposite Mather Point (about 4 miles/6.5km north of the south entrance station). North Rim Visitor Center: opposite parking lot on Bright Angel Peninsula
🕐 South Rim Visitor Center: daily 8–5 (longer during peak times). North Rim Visitor Center: mid-May to mid-Oct daily 8–6
❓ It is best to take an organized tour. Many companies offer bus, helicopter and light aircraft trips from Las Vegas

GRAND CANYON

To stand on the rim of the Grand Canyon and look down to its floor a mile below is to be confronted with raw nature at its most awe-inspiring. It's a sight from which any number of neck-craning fellow tourists can never detract.

The Grand Canyon stretches some 277 miles (446km) along the course of the Colorado River, and it is this mighty river that created it, eroding the landscape over a period of 5 million years. This erosion has revealed layer upon twisted layer of limestone, sandstone and shale, a fascinating geological cross-section of the earth's crust. At its widest point it's 17 miles (27km) from one side to the other and its deepest point is 1 mile (1.6km) beneath the rim.

The South Rim, 260 miles (418km) from Las Vegas, is the more touristy side of the canyon, and this is because it's more accessible, with an airport and rail depot. Grand Canyon Village here also has lots of visitor facilities, including hotels, restaurants, shops and museums. In addition, this is the start point for treks down into the canyon; if you have the energy this is a wonderful way to appreciate the topography to the full.

If you really want to get away from the crowds and experience the vast emptiness of the canyon, head for the incredibly spectacular North Rim, about 275 miles (443km) from Las Vegas in the dense forest of the Kaibab Plateau. If you want to visit both the North Rim and South Rim, you will need to figure into your travel plans the additional 200 miles (320km) it takes to get from one side to the other.

Excursions

VALLEY OF FIRE STATE PARK

Nevada's first state park takes its name from its red sandstone rock formations, formed millions of years ago by a shift in the earth's crust and eroded by water and wind.

The resulting weird and wonderful shapes resemble everything from elephants to pianos. Note the ancient rock art (*petroglyphs*) by the prehistoric Basketmaker people and Anasazi Pueblo farmers, who are thought to be North America's earliest inhabitants living along the Muddy River between 300BC and AD1150. The park also offers an opportunity to enjoy activities such as hiking, rock hunting, camping and picnicking. The visitor center provides trail maps and information.

THE BASICS

www.parks.nv.gov/vf
Distance: 55 miles (88km) northeast of Las Vegas
Journey Time: one hour
✉ Visitor Center: SR169 in Overton
☎ 702/397-2088
🕐 Daily 8.30–4.30
🅿 Parking inexpensive
❓ Take an organized tour or go by car via I-15 from Las Vegas

MOUNT CHARLESTON

Only a short drive away and always cooler than Las Vegas—by as much as 40°F (22°C)—this lovely alpine wilderness is an absolute joy to visit.

Located in the Spring Mountains, Charleston's peak reaches 11,900ft (3,628m). Together with the surrounding Toiyabe Forest, it is popular for hiking (52 miles/84km of trails), picnicking and camping. Nearby Lee Canyon is a great spot for skiing. Thick bristlecone pines cling to the limestone cliffs forming an awesome backdrop. The US Forest Service maintains the marked trails, which are suitable for all abilities. At the top of Kyle Canyon is the Mount Charleston Lodge, where you can enjoy good food and live entertainment in front of an open fire, with breathtaking views. When there is enough snow, horse-drawn sleighs leave from here.

THE BASICS

Distance: 35 miles (56km) northwest of Las Vegas
Journey Time: 30 min
❓ Take an organized tour or go by car (check road conditions in winter). From Las Vegas, take I-15 west and continue to US95 north. Stay on 95 until Kyle Canyon Road, then follow signs to Mount Charleston

FARTHER AFIELD

EXCURSIONS

Valley of Fire State Park

Shopping

BOULEVARD MALL
www.boulevardmall.com
The oldest mall in Vegas, popular with customers in the southeast part of the city for its moderate price tags. More than 150 shops, including department stores JC Penney, Macy's and Sears.
⊞ H8 ⊠ 3528 Maryland Parkway ☎ 702/732-8949
🚌 109

CHINATOWN PLAZA
www.lvchinatown.com
More than 25 vendors can be found in this red-roof Asian shopping mall, selling ceramics, clothing and handmade furniture.
⊞ Off map ⊠ 4255 Spring Mountain Road ☎ 702/221-8448 🚌 203

GALLERIA AT SUNSET
www.galleriaatsunset.com
Southeast of Downtown, the 140-plus shops here sell everything from shoes and clothing to electronics and home furnishings. Its anchors are JC Penney, Dillard's, Mervyn's California and Robinsons-May.
⊞ Off map ⊠ 1300 West Sunset Boulevard, Henderson ☎ 702/434-2409 🚌 212

HARLEY-DAVIDSON
www.lvhd.com
This Harley heaven, the largest Harley-Davidson store in the world, has gleaming machines on show and is full to the brim with Harley merchandise. If you can't afford to buy, you can rent a bike.

⊞ J6 ⊠ 2605 South Eastern Avenue ☎ 702/431-8500
🚌 110

JANA'S JADE GALLERY
This gallery sells an unusual and fascinating selection of hand-crafted jade jewelry.
⊞ Off map ⊠ Chinatown Plaza, 4255 Spring Mountain Road ☎ 702/227-9198
🚌 203

MEADOWS MALL
www.meadowsmall.com
Yet another huge mall made up of more than 140 main-street names and department stores.
⊞ B2 ⊠ 4300 Meadows Lane (at intersection of Valley View and US95) ☎ 702/878-4849 🚌 103, 104

Entertainment and Nightlife

ANGEL PARK GOLF CLUB
www.angelpark.com
Experience both mountains and palms at this 36-hole course designed by legendary golfer Arnold Palmer. There are views over Red Rock Canyon.
⊞ Off map ⊠ 100 South Rampart Boulevard, west of US95 at Summerlin Parkway ☎ 702/254-4653

LAS VEGAS NATIONAL
www.lasvegasnational.com
Opened in 1961, this

classic 18-hole golf course has glistening lakes. In 1996, champion golfer Tiger Woods won his first PGA victory here.
⊞ J7 ⊠ 1911 Desert Inn Road ☎ 702/734-1796
🚌 112

ORLEANS ARENA
www.orleansarena.com
Since opening in 2004, this huge arena has hosted Disney on Ice, top concerts and a variety of sporting events.
⊞ A10 ⊠ Orleans, 4500 West Tropicana ☎ 702/

365-SHOW; tickets 702/284-7777 🚌 201

ROYAL LINKS GOLF CLUB
www.royallinksgolfclub.com
This course has holes based on holes from famous British Open courses. In keeping with the British theme, the 18th hole looks like a medieval castle.
⊞ Off map ⊠ 5995 East Vegas Valley Road, 6 miles (10km) east ☎ 702/450-8000

A big part of the Las Vegas experience is to stay in one of the resort hotels. There is an endless supply of hotel rooms in the city and most of the biggest hotels in the world are here.

Introduction

Las Vegas is one of the few cities in the world where you can eat, drink, shop and be entertained without even needing to leave your hotel.

Hotels

For a truly unique experience, stay in one of the theme casino hotels on and around the Strip. These are like no others in the world and give you the added benefit of being right in the heart of the action. An increasing number of smaller, more exclusive hotels are popping up that offer an alternative for those who want time out away from the neon jungle. The north end of the Strip has seen better days in places. Some bastions of the "Golden Era" remain and have undergone extensive renovations, while others are gradually being torn down to make way for dazzling new resorts. If you want a taste of nostalgia, choose a hotel in historic downtown, which still remains a favorite with millions of visitors.

Motels

Las Vegas boasts dozens of motels near the Strip and downtown. Rates can be rock-bottom and their rooms are normally the last to get booked up, making them a good bet for finding a last-minute room. Motels don't have casinos, which also means they don't have large crowds. Don't expect much more than standard motel lodgings, but if you are on a tight budget and only require a clean, comfortable place to sleep, the motel is ideal.

GETTING THE BEST DEAL

For the best deal start looking well in advance: In Las Vegas it really does pay to shop around. Set a budget, know where you would like to stay and in what type of accommodations. Generally, prices are lower during the week but room rates fluctuate according to demand—they can change from day to day. Check to see if the city is staging a major convention before deciding when to go, as accommodations will be in demand, making prices higher. If you do your homework first, it's possible to get a luxury hotel room at a budget price.

Las Vegas tempts you to live in the lap of luxury with prices you can't refuse

Budget Hotels

PRICES

Expect to pay under $120 per night for a double room in a budget hotel.

BALLY'S LAS VEGAS

www.ballylasvegas.com
More sedate than many Vegas hotels, Bally's is less oriented toward a lively young crowd or families. The 2,814 rooms and 265 suites are sumptuous, with grand sitting rooms and opulent bathrooms. Floodlit tennis courts.

➕ D9 ✉ 3645 Las Vegas Boulevard South ☎ 702/739-4111; fax 702/967-4405 🚇 Bally's/Paris 🚍 Deuce; Strip trolley

CIRCUS CIRCUS (▷ 72)

www.circuscircus.com
Although it is one of the oldest hotels on the Strip, after recent refurbishments Circus Circus still provides one of the best value-for-money options if you have kids with you. It has 3,743 rooms and 130 suites.

➕ E6 ✉ 2880 Las Vegas Boulevard South ☎ 702/734-0410; fax 702/734-2268 🚍 Deuce; Strip trolley

FAIRFIELD INN BY MARRIOTT

www.fairfieldinn.com
Only 2 blocks east of the Strip, this pristine, small—in Vegas terms—hotel has a contemporary design. The 129 family rooms have a living area and are decorated in bright,

cheerful hues. Start your day with the "Early Eats" complimentary breakfast. Outdoor swimming pool and fitness center.

➕ F8 ✉ 3850 Paradise Road ☎ 702/791-0899; fax 702/791-2705 🚍 108

FLAMINGO LAS VEGAS

www.flamingolasvegas.com
Bugsy Siegel's original 1946 Flamingo was rebuilt by the Hilton group in 1993. The modern hotel has 3,565 units in all; the deluxe king rooms are spacious. The Flamingo also has one of the best pool areas on the Strip.

➕ D9 ✉ 3555 Las Vegas Boulevard South ☎ 702/733-3111; fax 702/862-3567 🚇 Flamingo/Caesars 🚍 Deuce; Strip trolley

HAWTHORN SUITES

www.hawthorn.com
An appealing alternative if

BEST OF BOTH WORLDS

With so much to do and see in Las Vegas, you probably won't be spending much time in your hotel room. In view of this—and the fact that most hotel rooms look pretty much the same—it might not make sense to pay out for an expensive room just for sleeping and storing your luggage. It is perfectly possible to stay in a lower price hotel, but spend your waking hours in the fancier establishments.

you prefer some distance between you and the Strip, but not too far off the beaten track. A good choice for families; the suites are plain but have kitchens and a balcony, and lots of extras.

➕ Off map ✉ 910 Boulder Highway, Henderson ☎ 702/568-7800; fax 702/568-8430 🚍 217

MAIN STREET STATION

www.mainstreetcasino.com
This characterful hotel has a Victorian theme, with genuine antiques, flickering gas lamps, iron railings and stained-glass windows. 406 bright rooms.

➕ G2 ✉ 200 North Main Street ☎ 702/387-1896; fax 702/388-2696 🚍 108

SOMERSET HOUSE

Handy for the Convention Center, and one block off the Strip, this good-value motel has 104 rooms and minisuites.

➕ E5 ✉ 294 Convention Center Drive ☎ 702/735-4411; fax 702/369-2388 🚇 Las Vegas Convention Center 🚍 108, Deuce; Strip trolley

TERRIBLE'S

www.terribleherbst.com
Don't be fooled by the name, as this small hotel near the Strip is anything but terrible. The 374 pleasant rooms are basic but clean, at very agreeable rates.

➕ F9 ✉ 4100 Paradise Road ☎ 702/733-7000; fax 702/691-2415 🚍 108

Mid-Range Hotels

ALEXIS PARK

www.alexispark.com
If you prefer to stay off the Strip, this small hotel, with 495 rooms, has some great two-level suites for a really good price. It's also fairly quiet here. Facilities include a spa.

🔲 E9　✉ 375 East Harmon Avenue　☎ 702/796-3300; fax 702/796-0766　🚌 108

COURTYARD BY MARRIOT

www.courtyard.com/LASCH
Part of the well-known chain, this hotel provides 149 nicer-than-the-average motel rooms (including 12 suites).

🔲 F7　✉ 3275 Paradise Road　☎ 702/791-3600; fax 702/796-7981　🚌 108

EMERALD SUITES – LAS VEGAS BLVD

www.emeraldsuites.com
On the Strip south of the Mandalay Bay, this non-gaming establishment features 396 suites, both one and two bedrooms, each tastefully decorated and equipped with a fully fitted kitchen. Guests have use of a lagoon-style pool nestled in pleasant landscaping.

🔲 Off map　✉ 9145 Las Vegas Boulevard South　☎ 702/948-9999; fax 702/948-9998　🚌 117

EXCALIBUR (▷ 24)

www.excalibur.com
Kids love this medieval castle, with its moat and drawbridge. Parents might find it all just a little tacky, but it's probably the best deal on the Strip, and has 3,991 comfortable, peaceful rooms.

🔲 D10　✉ 3850 Las Vegas Boulevard South　☎ 702/597-7777; fax 702/597-7009　🚌 Deuce; Strip trolley

HOOTERS

www.hooterscasinohotel.com
It's all surfboards and palm trees at this recently remodeled casino-hotel.

THE HOTEL EXPERIENCE

The fanciful hotel architecture of Las Vegas means that many people come here for the hotel experience alone. Some rarely leave the premises—quite understandable when there's an on-site casino, a choice of superb restaurants, world-class shows and shopping, luxury spas and plenty of other leisure amenities. On the downside, the large hotels can suffer from slow service and long lines for checking in and out, though express check-out boxes are available in many cases. You simply drop off your keys and leave, and your credit card is charged about a week later. If you are going to stay in a very large hotel, try to get a room near the elevator.

Floridian-style bedrooms, some in a bungalow building separate from the main towers, are bright and sunny. Hooters is more intimate than some of the Vegas giants and has a fun atmosphere and friendly staff.

🔲 D10　✉ 115 East Tropicana　☎ 702/739-9000; fax 702/739-7783　🚌 201

HOWARD JOHNSON –LAS VEGAS STRIP

www.howardjohnson lasvegasstrip.com
This low-rise motel is in a good location at the north end of the Strip. Some of the 100 rooms have a whirlpool bath.

🔲 F5　✉ 1401 Las Vegas Boulevard South　☎ 702/388-0301; fax 702/388-2506　🚌 Deuce; Strip trolley

LAS VEGAS HILTON

www.lvhilton.com
This old-timer still offers fine accommodations in its 3,500 guest rooms, with individual opulent style. Elvis staged his comeback here in 1969 to 1977 (note the statue at the entrance), and the hotel was used in the Bond film *Diamonds are Forever*.

🔲 F7　✉ 3000 Paradise Road　☎ 702/732-5111; fax 702/732-5805　🚊 Las Vegas Hilton　🚌 108

LUXOR

www.luxor.com
This 4,411-room, pyramid-shape hotel is Egyptian-theme right down to its foundations.

You enter beneath a huge sphinx and are taken to your room via an elevator that travels up the pyramid's slope.
➕ D11 ✉ 3900 Las Vegas Boulevard South ☎ 702/262-4000; fax 702/262-4452 🚍 Deuce; Strip trolley

MGM GRAND
www.mgmgrand.com
This is pure Hollywood, with figures of stars dotted around the lobby and huge stills from movies on the walls. The 5,000-plus rooms offer a range of options, from the small Emerald Tower rooms to spacious suites.
➕ D10 ✉ 3799 Las Vegas Boulevard South ☎ 702/891-1111; fax 702/891-7272 🚇 MGM Grand 🚍 Deuce; Strip trolley

MONTE CARLO (▷ 35)
www.montecarlo.com
A popular choice with golfers (it has a full-time golf concierge), the Monte Carlo has 3,000-or-so attractive rooms and suites.
➕ D10 ✉ 3770 Las Vegas Boulevard South ☎ 702/730-7777; fax 702/730-7250 🚍 Deuce; Strip trolley

NEW YORK-NEW YORK (▷ 31)
www.nynyhotelcasino.com
Love it or hate it, this huge mock-up of the New York skyline is an experience to stay at. The 2,023 rooms are in a sophisticated '40s-style decorated in earth tones

and pastels with dark rich wood furniture. Light sleepers should request a room away from the roller-coaster that trundles around the outside.
➕ D10 ✉ 3790 Las Vegas Boulevard South ☎ 702/740-6969; fax 702/740-6875 🚍 Deuce; Strip trolley

RIO ALL-SUITE HOTEL
www.playrio.com
This is a lively hotel in an off-Strip location, with great nightlife and two excellent buffets among its dining options. It has 2,548 huge suites.
➕ B8 ✉ 3700 Flamingo Road ☎ 702/777-7777; fax 702/777-7611 🚍 202

PALMS RESORT
www.palms.com
As the name suggests,

HOTEL TIPPING
As in any US city, it is customary to offer a gratuity to hotel employees for prompt and courteous service. Las Vegas has a huge amount of different staff who provide such services, and who gets what can be confusing. The amount is at the customer's discretion but here are some general guidelines: Bell captains and bellhops $1–$2 per bag; hotel maids $2 per day upon departure; valets $2; use of concierge or VIP services $5; waiters and waitresses 15 to 20 percent of the bill.

expect plenty of tropical foliage at this towering hotel. The Palms' hot-spot reputation is due mainly to the clientele its night-time haunts, such as the Ghost Bar (▷ 64), attract. The 700 bedrooms are luxurious, with extra fluffy pillows and duvets, and huge bathrooms.
➕ B9 ✉ 4321 West Flamingo Road ☎ 702/942-7777; fax 702/942-7001 🚍 202

TREASURE ISLAND
www.treasureisland.com
Rocks, cliffs and a lagoon at the front of this sophisticated resort set the scene for the Caribbean island theme inside. The 3,000 good-size rooms and suites, decorated in French Regency style, have floor-to-ceiling windows—Strip side, there's no better view of the Sirens of Ti pirate battle (▷ 61).
➕ D8 ✉ 3300 Las Vegas Boulevard South ☎ 702/894-7111; fax 702/894-7446 🚍 Deuce; Strip trolley

THE VENETIAN (▷ 56)
www.venetian.com
Famous for its canals and replica of St. Mark's Square, the Venetian has 4,027 rooms (actually they are all suites). The decor varies, although all have marble bathrooms and fine furnishings.
➕ D8 ✉ 3355 Las Vegas Boulevard South ☎ 702/414-1000; fax 702/414-4805 🚍 Deuce; Strip trolley

Luxury Hotels

BELLAGIO (▷ 46)

www.bellagio.com
Set behind an enormous lake, this is one of the most beautiful hotels in Vegas, built in the style of a huge Mediterranean villa with lovely gardens. The 4,000-plus rooms and suites are large and classy, decorated in natural hues.

✚ D9 ⊠ 3600 Las Vegas Boulevard South ☎ 702/693-7111; fax 702/693-8559 🚌 Deuce; Strip trolley

CAESARS PALACE (▷ 47)

www.caesarspalace.com
Ancient Rome prevails through classical temples, marble columns and every possible excess you can imagine. All 3,348 rooms and 189 suites are luxurious, but even more so in the tower, where there are huge whirlpool tubs in the bathrooms.

✚ D8 ⊠ 3570 Las Vegas Boulevard South ☎ 702/731-7110; fax 702/8-170066 🚌 Deuce; Strip trolley

FOUR SEASONS LAS VEGAS

www.fourseasons.com
This hotel takes up the top five levels of the Mandalay Bay, but retains its own tranquil identity. The 424 rooms and suites are elegantly decorated in peach, aqua and gold, and all the Mandalay Bay facilities are available to guests.

✚ D11 ⊠ 3960 Las Vegas Boulevard South ☎ 702/632-5000; fax 702/632-5222 🚌 Deuce; Strip trolley

MANDALAY BAY

www.mandalaybay.com
There is masses of big-city style at the Mandalay Bay. It's the only hotel in Las Vegas with a beach and a gigantic wave pool. There are 3,000-plus rooms and suites; even the standard rooms are huge, and all are light and airy.

✚ D11 ⊠ 3950 Las Vegas Boulevard South ☎ 702/632-7228; fax 702/632-7190 🚌 Deuce; Strip trolley

PLATINUM HOTEL AND SPA

www.theplatinumhotel.com
Opened July 2006, this non-gaming retreat is in lavish contemporary style.

HOTEL GRADING

US hotels, including those in Las Vegas, are classified by the American Automobile Association (AAA, or Triple A) into five categories, from one to five diamonds. As this is based entirely on facilities offered, it does mean that hotels with four diamonds can be equally as luxurious as those with five, or that an attractively furnished atmospheric two-diamond bed-and-breakfast may cost less than a down-at-heel three-diamond business hotel.

Spacious all-suite rooms have a kitchen, whirlpool tubs and a balcony overlooking the Strip or mountains. You can indulge in the soothing spa, and there is an indoor and outdoor pool.

✚ D9 ⊠ 211 East Flamingo Road ☎ 702/365-5000; fax 702/365-5001 🚌 202

RENAISSANCE LAS VEGAS

www.renaissancelasvegas.com
For a retreat from the Vegas clamor and commotion, the Renaissance has cool and confident style without a slot machine in sight. The 580 rooms and suites are richly decorated and have a calming feel. Spa and health club.

✚ F8 ⊠ 3400 Paradise Road ☎ 702/733-6533; fax 702/735-3288 🚇 Las Vegas Convention Center 🚌 108

WYNN LAS VEGAS (▷ 79)

www.wynnlasvegas.com
Steve Wynn's latest incredible hotel-casino is the world's most expensive hotel, and occupies 60 floors. The 3,716-plus rooms are huge and very stylish, and are equipped with every conceivable luxury. There is a private lake, man-made mountain and an 18-hole golf course.

✚ E7 ⊠ 3131 Las Vegas Boulevard South ☎ 702/770-7100; fax 702/770-1571 🚇 Las Vegas Convention Center 🚌 Deuce; Strip trolley

A trip to Las Vegas can be hectic so it is best to organize as much as you can before you leave. The following information will help in planning transportation, reserving tours and anything else that will help you to have a successful visit.

Need to Know

Planning Ahead

When to Go

With so many of its attractions under cover and not dependent on weather conditions, there's no off-season to speak of in Las Vegas. Avoid high summer if you don't like excessively hot weather, unless you plan to stay indoors.

TIME

Vegas is on Pacific Standard Time (GMT –8), advanced one hour between early April and early October.

AVERAGE DAILY MAXIMUM TEMPERATURES

JAN	FEB	MAR	APR	MAY	JUN	JUL	AUG	SEP	OCT	NOV	DEC
56°F	62°F	68°F	78°F	88°F	98°F	104°F	102°F	94°F	81°F	66°F	57°F
13°C	17°C	20°C	25°C	31°C	36°C	40°C	39°C	34°C	27°C	19°C	14°C

Summer (June to September) can be incredibly hot and oppressive, with daytime temperatures sometimes soaring as high as 49°C (120°F).

Spring and autumn are much more comfortable, with average temperatures usually reaching 70°F (21°C).

Winter (December to February) sees average temperatures above 10°C (50°F). There can be the odd chillier day when you will need a jacket, and sometimes it can drop below freezing at night.

WHAT'S ON

January *Laughlin Desert Challenge*: Top drivers compete in an off-road motor race over rough terrain.

March *NASCAR Nextel Cup Race* (early Mar): A major event on the racing calendar, held at the Las Vegas Motor Speedway.

St. Patrick's Day Parade (Mar 17): A parade of floats downtown kicks off other entertainment; Celtic bands, storytellers and dancers.

June *CineVegas International Film Festival* (early Jun): Film debuts from studios, with celebrities attending the huge parties.

Jul/Aug *World Series of Poker*: The world's best poker players compete for supremacy at Harrah's Rio.

September *International Mariachi Festival*: A popular Mexican festival that takes place in the Aladdin Theatre.

October *Frys.com Open*: A major week-long golf tournament played on two of the city's best courses.

November *Comedy Festival*: A 5-day festival in multiple venues throughout Caesars Palace, with dozens of performers and special events.

December *National Finals Rodeo* (early Dec): During the 10-day finals, cowboys compete and the rest of the city goes country-mad, dressing up, line-dancing and feasting on barbecues.

New Year's Eve Celebrations: A party held at Fremont Street.

Billboard Music Awards: Music celebrities gather at the MGM Grand Garden Arena to honor the world's best music.

First Friday A huge arts and entertainment party takes place on the first Friday of each month in the Arts District downtown (✉ 702/384-0092; www.firstfriday-lasvegas.org ⏰ 6–10pm).

Las Vegas Online

www.vegasfreedom.com
The official website of the Las Vegas Convention and Visitors Bureau offers well-presented information on everything you could possibly need to know when planning your trip to Las Vegas.

www.lasvegas.com
For articles on local news, listings, events and other sources of information, try this useful site run by the respected *Review Journal*, Nevada's largest newspaper.

www.vegas.com
This informative site geared to visitors has honest reviews of restaurants, bars, shows and nightlife, plus it gives access to hotel booking.

www.lasvegasgolf.com
To help you plan a golfing holiday in Las Vegas, this site has detailed reviews on all the courses open in Vegas and other US cities.

www.vegasexperience.com
This lively site is dedicated to the Fremont Street Experience. See what's going on at any time of the year and look for places to stay and eat.

www.gayvegas.com
The most complete site for gay locals and visitors to Las Vegas. It keeps up with the latest information on clubs, bars, restaurants and organizations, plus lots more.

www.nightonthetown.com
For one of the most comprehensive and easy-to-use guides to eating out in Las Vegas, check out this site. The restaurants are listed under cuisine type and location.

www.cheapovegas.com
Geared to the visitor who wants to do Vegas on a budget, this fun guide provides comprehensive reviews and unbiased opinions with a humorous slant.

PRIME TRAVEL SITES

www.CATRIDE.com
Official site for the Citizens Area Transit (CAT), the company responsible for the Las Vegas bus system. Operate the fun route planner to discover exactly how to get from A to B.

www.fodors.com
A complete travel-planning site where you can research prices and weather; book air tickets, cars and rooms; pose questions (and get answers) to fellow visitors; and find links to other sites.

INTERNET CAFÉS

Most hotels in Las Vegas have business centers and offer internet access to their guests. www.netcafeguide.com and www.cybercafes.com are up-to-date search engines enabling you to locate internet cafés all over the world.

Cyber Stop Internet Café
www.cyberstopinc.com
✉ 3743 Las Vegas Boulevard South (opposite the Monte Carlo) ☎ 702/496-3678 🕐 Daily 9–8
💲 30 mins $8, 1 hour $12

Getting There

ENTRY REQUIREMENTS

All visitors require a valid passport, and all except Canadians must have an onward ticket. Visas may not be needed by UK, Irish, Canadian, Australian, New Zealand or other EU nationals staying less than three months—check with the embassy in your home country before leaving. Health and accident insurance is required.

AIRPORT FACTS

● McCarran airport has two clean and well-organized terminals with more than 50 retail shops and nearly 30 restaurants and snack bars.
● This huge modern airport has had a $500 million expansion.
● 36 million passengers per year pass through the airport.
● It is among the 15 busiest airports in the world.
● This is one of only a few airports where you can play the slot machines in the terminals while waiting for your luggage, or work out in a 24-hour fitness center.

AIRPORT

McCarran International Airport (LAS) is served by direct flights from cities right across North America, and there are intercontinental flights from London, Frankfurt and Tokyo. It is worth checking for special deals from airline and flight brokers, in newspapers and on the internet.

19km (12 miles)
13km (8 miles)
6km (4 miles)

McCarran International Airport

FROM MCCARRAN INTERNATIONAL AIRPORT

The McCarran airport terminal (☎ 702/261-5211; www.mccarran.com) is 4 miles (6km) southeast of the Strip, at 5757 Wayne Newton Boulevard. There is a ground Transportation Center near baggage claim for shuttles and for renting cars and limousines and there are also information desks throughout the airport if you need assistance.

Many different companies run airport shuttle buses every 10 or 15 minutes from just outside the baggage claim area—leave through door No. 12. They all cost roughly the same (about $5.50 to the Strip and $7 to Downtown) and normally operate 24 hours. Most stop at all the major hotels and motels. Advance reservations for shuttles ☎ 702/558-9155. Check first, as your resort hotel might offer an airport shuttle. Less expensive are the CAT buses (about $2) that operate from outside the airport terminal: No. 108 will take you to the Las Vegas Hilton, from where you can transfer to the Deuce (▷ 118), which stops close to most hotels along the Strip; and No. 109 goes to the Downtown Transportation Center.

Taxis are also easily available outside baggage claim, and cost $9–$13 to the Strip, or $16–$19 to Downtown hotels. Stretch limos line up outside the airport waiting to take you to your destination; if you are tempted, try to share as they can be costly ($35–$45 per hour). Try Ambassador Limousines (☎ 702/362-6200) or Las Vegas Limousines (☎ 702/736-1419). For those wishing to rent a car, all major car rental companies are represented inside the airport's arrival hall (▷ panel). There are buses and shuttles available to take you to the rental company you are using. It is better to reserve a car in advance.

ARRIVING BY BUS

Greyhound/Trailways (www.greyhound.com) operates services to Las Vegas from most cities and towns in California and Nevada. Tickets can normally be purchased just prior to departure. This is a convenient and inexpensive way to travel, although probably not the most comfortable. All Greyhound buses arrive at Downtown's bus terminal at 200 South Main Street (☎ 702/384-9561).

ARRIVING BY CAR

Interstate 15 from Los Angeles to Vegas takes you through some of the most breathtaking scenery of the Mojave Desert. The journey takes 4–5 hours depending on road, weather and traffic conditions (delays are often caused by construction work). Carry plenty of water and a spare tire, and keep an eye on your fuel level.

ARRIVING BY RAIL

Amtrak (www.amtrak.com), the national train company, does not offer a direct service to Las Vegas, but you can connect to the city by bus from other rail destinations in California and Arizona. Amtrak has talked of restoring the line from Los Angeles to Las Vegas, but at the time of writing nothing had materialized. Contact Amtrak (☎ 800/872-7245; www.amtrak.com) for the latest details.

CAR RENTAL

Hotel information desks can advise about renting a car. Rental companies will deliver to your hotel and pick up again at the end of the rental period.

Avis	702/261-5595
Budget	702/736-1212
Enterprise	702/795-8842
Hertz	702/262-7700
National	702/261-5391
Thrifty	702/896-7600

CUSTOMS

● Visitors from outside the US, age 21 or over, may import duty-free: 200 cigarettes, or 50 non-Cuban cigars, or 2kg of tobacco; 1 liter of alcohol; and gifts up to $100 in value.

● The import of wildlife souvenirs sourced from rare or endangered species may either be illegal or require a special permit. Before purchase you should check your home country's customs regulations.

● Restricted import items include meat, seeds, plants and fruit.

● Some medication bought over the counter abroad may be prescription-only in the US and could be confiscated. Bring a doctor's certificate for essential medication.

Getting Around

VISITORS WITH DISABILITIES

If you are a wheelchair-user, on arrival at the airport you will find shuttle buses with wheelchair lifts to get you into the city. You will also find easy access to most restaurants, showrooms and lounges. All the hotel casinos have accessible slot machines, and many provide access to table games. Assisted listening devices are also widely available. If you plan to rent a car, you can request a free 90-day disabled parking permit, which can be used through-out Vegas; contact the City of Las Vegas Parking Permit Office (☎ 702/229-6431).

Las Vegas Convention and Visitors Authority ADA coordinator
☎ 702/892-0711

WALKING

The Strip is 3.5 miles (5.5km) long, and it's a taxing walk in the heat. Wear comfortable shoes and sunglasses. Even if you use the Strip's transporta-tion, you will still have to walk considerable distances to and from the hotels and attrac-tions. Overhead walkways connect several places along the Strip. Make a note of the cross streets that punctuate the Strip to help you get your bearings; some are named after the hotels along them.

Most of what you will want to see and do in Las Vegas is found along Las Vegas Boulevard, which is well served by buses. The boulevard is divided into two parts: Downtown, between Charleston Boulevard and Washington Avenue; and the Strip, comprising several long blocks—Sahara, Spring Mountain, Flamingo, Tropicana and Russell. Hotels on the Strip (between Hacienda Avenue and the Sahara Hotel) are also served by red and green Las Vegas Strip Trolleys, and in 2004 the first leg of a new multimillion dollar monorail was launched, providing a welcome addition to the options for getting up and down the Strip.

BUSES

CAT (Citizens Area Transit ☎ 702/228-7433) runs 51 bus routes throughout the entire system, of which 24 operate 24-hours a day. The Downtown Transportation Center (DTC) at Casino Center Boulevard and South Strip Transfer Terminal (SSTT) at Gillespie Street are major transfer points. The Deuce provides transportation along the Strip from the DTC to the SSTT, with many stops along the way, and runs about every 10 minutes (during peak times) 24 hours a day. The double-decker bus, launched in 2005, accommodates 97 people. The fare is $2 one-way or $5 for a day pass, which you can purchase on the bus or from vending machines (you need to have the exact fare because drivers can't give change). You can get a transfer from the driver for off-Strip destinations, so you don't have to pay again. Off-strip buses otherwise cost $1.25 one-way. Hotels should have timetables for the citywide system; if not, call the number above.

DRIVING

Almost every hotel on Las Vegas Boulevard South has its own self-parking garage. The best way into them, avoiding the gridlock on the Strip, is via the back entrances. Valet parking is also available at the front (and sometimes other) entrances. The standard tip for valets is

$2 if they are particularly speedy. The best advice about driving in Las Vegas is don't do it unless you really have to. The speed limit on the Strip is 35mph (56kph). The wearing of seat belts is compulsory.

MONORAILS
The eagerly awaited state-of-the-art monorail (www.lvmonorail.com) opened in 2004. Running from MGM Grand to the Sahara, it operates every day from 7pm to 2am (Fri, Sat until 3am). There are seven stations: MGM Grand, Bally's/Paris, Flamingo/Caesars, Harrah's/Imperial Palace, Las Vegas Convention Center, Las Vegas Hilton and Sahara. A single fare costs $5, a two-ride ticket $9, a 10-ride ticket is $35, a one-day pass is $15 and a three-day pass costs $40. There are also a number of smaller free monorail services courtesy of the hotels, including one between the Mandalay Bay, the Excalibur and the Luxor (4am–2am), and one between the Bellagio and Monte Carlo (24 hours).

TAXIS AND LIMOUSINES
Taxis line up outside every hotel and you can call for one from your room. If you are already out, you need to call or go to a cab stand; taxis can't be hailed in the street. Taxi drivers are a good source of information. They have first-hand experience of all the shows and attractions, and can offer a review and make recommendations. For this service you should give more of a tip than the standard $1 or $2 for a straightforward journey. Also give a bigger tip if they help with the door and your luggage. There are plenty of limousine services, which start at $35 per hour. Your hotel concierge can make the necessary arrangements.

TROLLEYS
The trolley (☎ 702/382-1404) plies the Strip from 9.30am to 1.30am, stopping at major hotels along the boulevard every 15 minutes. You need to have the exact fare of $1.75.

ORGANIZED SIGHTSEEING
There is no shortage of Vegas-based tour companies offering trips from Vegas to wherever you want to go, but there are also plenty showing the best of the city sights. These tours can give you an insider's view on city attractions, along with a good overview and orientation, before you start exploring independently. Nearly every hotel in Las Vegas has a sightseeing desk from where you can book tours. If the tour bus approach doesn't appeal to you, there are all kinds of other options, including small-scale specialized tours with your own group of family or friends, or using a limousine to whisk you from place to place. Perhaps best of all, you can take to the skies in a helicopter for a bird's-eye view of the fantastic architecture and, on after-dark flights, the glittering lights. The Nitelife Tour Company's (☎ www.nitetourslasvegas.com) nightclub tours, also after dark, will transport you to the current most popular dance and Latin clubs. The company also offers a Las Vegas microbreweries tour. Other reputable tour companies include: Scenic Airlines (www.scenic.com) and Look Tours (www.looktours.com).

Essential Facts

MEDICAL TREATMENT

In medical emergencies call ☎ 911 or go to the casualty department of the nearest hospital. Emergency-room services are available 24 hours at University Medical Center (✉ 1800 West Charleston Boulevard ☎ 702/383-2000), or Sunrise Hospital and Medical Center (✉ 3186 Maryland Parkway ☎ 702/731-8000). Pharmacies are indicated by a large green or red cross. Pharmacy telephone numbers are listed under "Pharmacies" or "Drugstores" in the Yellow Pages. Many will deliver medication to your hotel. 24-hour and night pharmacies are available at Walgreens (✉ 1111 Las Vegas Boulevard ☎ 702/471-6840), and at Sav-On (✉ 2300 East Tropicana Avenue ☎ 702/458-1450).

ELECTRICITY
● Voltage is 110/120 volts AC (60 cycles) and sockets take two-prong, flat-pin plugs. European appliances also need a voltage transformer.

EMERGENCIES
Police ☎ 911.
Fire ☎ 911.
Ambulance ☎ 911.
American Automobile Association (AAA) breakdown service ☎ 800/222-4357.

ETIQUETTE
● Tip staff at least 15–20 percent in a restaurant, taxi drivers $1–$2 for a direct route, porters $1–$2 per bag depending on the distance carried, and valet parking attendants $2.
● Las Vegas is one of the few pro-smoking places left in the US. Most restaurants have designated smoking areas.
● Dress is very informal during the day, and shorts and T-shirts are generally accepted anywhere. In the evening, smart-casual is more the norm, and some lounges, nightclubs and restaurants may have a dress code.

GAMING
Nevada law permits a wide variety of gaming, but the most popular flutters are roulette, blackjack, craps and slot machines. If you are new to the game, take some time to watch before actually taking the plunge; you could pick up a few tips from the hard-and-fast gamblers. Punters have to be 21 to play. Most casinos do not have windows or clocks, so you are unaware of time passing, and they will often keep you refueled with free drinks and snacks. One benefit of all this cash changing hands is that most of the gaming taxes collected by the state are funneled into public education.

Glossary of terms:
Action Gaming activity measured by the amount wagered.

Bank The person covering the bets in any game, usually the casino.

Buy in Purchasing of chips.

Cage The cashier's section of the casino.

Even money A bet that pays off at one to one.

House edge The mathematical advantage the casino enjoys on every game and wager.

House odds The ratio at which the casino pays off a winning bet.

Limit The minimum/maximum bet accepted at a gambling table.

Loose machine A slot machine set to return a high percentage on the money you put in.

Marker An IOU owed to the casino by someone playing on credit.

Toke A tip or gratuity.

LOST PROPERTY

● For property lost on public transportation: ✉ 6675 South Strip Transfer Terminal, South Gillespie Street ☎ 702/228-7433 🕔 Mon–Fri 7–5.30.

● For property lost at McCarran International Airport: ☎ 702/261-5134 🕔 Daily 6.30am–1am.

● Report losses of passports or credit cards to the police.

NATIONAL HOLIDAYS

Jan 1: New Year's Day
3rd Mon in Jan: Martin Luther King Jr. Day
3rd Mon in Feb: President's Day
Mar/Apr: Easter (half-day holiday on Good Friday)
Last Mon in May: Memorial Day
Jul 4: Independence Day
1st Mon in Sep: Labor Day
2nd Mon in Oct: Columbus Day
Nov 11: Veterans' Day
4th Thu in Nov: Thanksgiving
Dec 25: Christmas Day

OPENING HOURS

● Banks: generally Mon–Fri 9–3 or later, and some Sat mornings.

MONEY

● Credit cards are widely accepted.
● Most banks have ATMs.
● US-dollar travelers' checks are accepted as cash in most places, but ID may be requested.
● Most major hotels will exchange foreign currency, and there are several exchange bureaus on the Strip. You can also change money at major banks.

CURRENCY

The unit of currency is the dollar ($), divided into 100 cents. Bills (notes) are in denominations of $1, $5, $10, $20, $50 and $100. Coins are 1 cent (penny), 5 cents (nickel), 10 cents (dime), 25 cents (quarter) and 50 cents (half dollar).

5 dollars

10 dollars

50 dollars

100 dollars

NEWSPAPERS AND MAGAZINES

● Las Vegas has two daily newspapers: the *Las Vegas Review Journal* and the *Las Vegas Sun*.
● Weeklies with club listings and restaurant and bar reviews include *City Life* and *Las Vegas Weekly*.

TELEPHONE

There are public payphones in hotels, casinos, stores, restaurants, gas stations and on many street corners. You will need a good supply of quarters (overseas calls cost at least $5.50). Local calls from a phone booth cost around 35 cents. Some phones are equipped to take prepaid phone cards and/or charge cards and credit cards. Dial 1 plus the area code for numbers within the United States and Canada. Calls made from hotel rooms are very expensive. Las Vegas' area code is 702, which does not need to be dialed if you are calling within the city. To call Las Vegas from the UK, dial 00 followed by 1 (the code for the US and Canada), then the number. To call the UK from Las Vegas, dial 00 44, then drop the first zero from the area code.

● Post offices: normally Mon–Fri 8.30–6, with limited hours on Sat.
● Stores: usually open at 10am; closing times vary, and may be later on weekends.
● Museums: see individual entries for details.
● Las Vegas boasts that it never closes and never sleeps, but off-Strip stores and banks, and peripheral businesses, will be closed on certain holidays.

POST OFFICES

● Main post office: ✉ 1001 East Sunset Road, between Paradise Road and Maryland Parkway ☎ 800/275-8777 🕐 Mon–Fri 7.30–9, Sat 8–4. There are many post offices in the city. You can also mail letters and parcels from your hotel.
● Buy stamps from shops and from machines.
● US mailboxes are red and white.

SENSIBLE PRECAUTIONS

Carry only as much money with you as you need; leave other cash and valuables in the hotel safe. At night, avoid hotel parking lots and always enter the hotel via the main entrance. If renting an apartment, use valet parking. Report theft or mugging on the street to the police department immediately. Make sure your room is locked when you leave. Locks can be changed regularly in hotels for security reasons.

STUDENT TRAVELERS

Discounts are sometimes available to students who have an International Student Identity Card (ISIC).

TOILETS

There is never a shortage of clean, free public restrooms to be found throughout the city in hotels, casinos, restaurants and bars.

TOURIST INFORMATION OFFICE

Las Vegas Visitor Information Center:
✉ 3150 Paradise Road, Las Vegas, NV 89109
☎ 702/892-0711; fax 702/892-2824;
www.vegasfreedom.com

Language

The official language of the USA is English, and, given the large number of visitors from the UK, Las Vegas residents have few problems coping with British accents and dialects. Spanish is also widely spoken, as many workers in the hotel and catering industries are of Latin origin. Some English words have different meanings in US and UK English. A selection is given below.

USEFUL WORDS	
shop	*store*
chemist (shop)	*drugstore*
cinema	*movie theater*
film	*movie*
pavement	*sidewalk*
subway	*underpass*
toilet	*restroom*
trousers	*pants*
nappy	*diaper*
glasses	*eyeglasses*
policeman	*cop*
post	*mail*
surname	*last name*
holiday	*vacation*
handbag	*purse*
cheque	*check*
banknote	*bill*
cashpoint	*automatic teller*
autumn	*fall*
ground floor	*first floor*
first floor	*second floor*
flat	*apartment*
lift	*elevator*
eiderdown	*comforter*
tap	*faucet*
luggage	*baggage*
suitcase	*trunk*
hotel porter	*bellhop*
chambermaid	*room maid*
cupboard	*closet*
car	*automobile*
bonnet	*hood*
boot	*trunk*
petrol	*gas*

FOOD	
grilled	*broiled*
prawns	*shrimp*
aubergine	*eggplant*
courgette	*zucchini*
chips	*fries*
crisps	*chips*
biscuit	*cookie*
scone	*biscuit*
jelly	*jello*
jam	*jelly*
sweets	*candy*
soft drink	*soda*

Timeline

EARLY BEGINNINGS

In prehistoric times the land on which the city stands was a marshy area that supported vigorous plant life, but the water eventually receded and the arid landscape we see today was created. However, underground water occasionally surfaced to nourish an oasis on the site where Vegas now stands, known at that time only to the area's Native Americans. Archaeological finds just 10 miles (16km) northwest of Vegas have identified one of the oldest sites of human habitation in the United States. Items found at Tule Springs date from around 11,000 to 14,000 years ago.

1829 The spring at Las Vegas is discovered by a Mexican scout, Rafael Rivera, riding with a 60-strong trading party that had strayed from the Spanish Trail en route to Los Angeles.

1855 Mormon settlers build a fort at Las Vegas. They stay for three years, until Native American raids drive them out.

1905 On May 15, the railroad arrives, and trackside lots in what is now the Fremont Street area sell like hot cakes.

1910 Gambling is made illegal in the state of Nevada, sending the games underground.

1931 The Nevada legislature passes a bill to allow gambling, and El Rancho becomes the first casino to open in Las Vegas. Nevada remains the only state to allow casino gambling until 1976, when casinos are introduced to Atlantic City.

1940s A building boom expands Las Vegas and more casinos come to town, along with organized crime. Vegas is ruled by the Mafia for decades.

1946 The Flamingo, one of the foremost early casinos, opens its doors. It was financed by Benjamin "Bugsy" Siegel of the Meyer Lansky gang.

1959 The Tropicana Hotel buys the American rights to the Parisian Folies

Bergère show—it's still running today with some 40,000 spectators a month.

1960s The Rat Pack (Frank Sinatra, Dean Martin, Sammy Davis Jr. et al.) come to Las Vegas, setting the pattern for superstar entertainment.

1966 Howard Hughes, pioneer aviator, billionaire and renowned recluse, takes up residence at the Desert Inn.

1967 The Nevada legislature approves a bill that allows publicly traded corporations to obtain gambling licenses. Legitimate money begins to loosen the Mafia's hold.

1976 Casino gambling is legalized in Atlantic City and, for the first time, Las Vegas has competition.

1990s Las Vegas begins to promote family attractions. Ever bigger, more fantastic architecture starts to dominate the Strip.

2001 Wayne Newton, "Mr Las Vegas," signs a lucrative contract with the Stardust Hotel.

2004 A new state-of-the art monorail opens.

2005 On May 15, Las Vegas celebrates its 100th birthday.

2007 Opened 1958, the legendary Stardust Hotel is the latest hotel to be demolished.

THE MORMON FORT

The first people to settle the area were not gamblers or casino owners—they were Mormons, who built a fort here in the mid-19th century. It became a welcome stopover for pioneers and traders on the Spanish Trail from Mexico to Los Angeles. The residents later turned to farming, but were driven out in 1858 when they'd had enough of the frequent raids by Native Americans. Today, the fort is open to the public, and you can see refurbished buildings and a re-created pioneer garden.

✉ 500 East Washington
☎ 702/486-3511 ⏱ Daily 8.30–3.30 💲 Inexpensive

From left to right: The Folies Bergère at the Tropicana; The Rat Pack hit the scene in the 1960s; Desert Inn, an old favorite no longer standing; the early days of gambling

Index